"Drawing on his experience as both a practicing church musician and a scholar, Cheung Salisbury deftly explores the relationship between worship today and its historical antecedents. He asks the important question of how worship, in each age, has appealed to the senses, what its function has been, and what it might still be. This fascinating and interdisciplinary work, which will appeal to people of faith or of none, impressively imparts insights from history, music, and liturgical practice in order to help us understand why we worship, what happens when we do, and what it is for. Cheung Salisbury shows us that, although the form of worship may have undergone change in different ages, its performative function is as relevant as ever, the constant thread being the objective of prayer and praise to God and the innate necessity for human beings to engage in God-directed activity."

Rev. Dr. Jonathan Arnold
Chaplain and Senior Research Fellow
Worcester College, Oxford

Matthew Cheung Salisbury

Hear My Voice, O God

Functional Dimensions of Christian Worship

A PUEBLO BOOK

Liturgical Press   Collegeville, Minnesota
www.litpress.org

A Pueblo Book published by Liturgical Press

Cover design by Jodi Hendrickson. Photo: Dreamstime.

1 2 3 4 5 6 7 8 9

Library of Congress Cataloging-in-Publication Data

Salisbury, Matthew Cheung.
Hear my voice, O God : functional dimensions of Christian worship / Matthew Cheung Salisbury.
pages cm
"A Pueblo book."
ISBN 978-0-8146-6307-3 — ISBN 978-0-8146-6332-5 (ebook)
1. Liturgics. I. Title.

BV176.3.S25 2014
264.009—dc23

2014000347

To students, past and present,
who have helped to ask the questions.

Contents

Acknowledgments ix

Introduction xi

1. "Full and Active Participation" 1

2. The Liturgical Movement 25

3. Reformations and the Council of Trent 55

4. The Later Middle Ages 88

5. "A School for the Lord's Service" 118

6. The Time of Jesus and the Early Church 139

Epilogue 158

Index 161

Acknowledgments

I am grateful for many discussions with students and colleagues, past and present, who encountered many of the questions posed in this book in their own studies, and who have helped me along in the task of writing. My own first explorations of liturgy and worship, guided by the late Professor Andrew Hughes and Fr. Daniel Donovan, are a point to which I often find myself returning, and I owe much to their teaching. I have been grateful for the support and encouragement of Professor John Harper and Dr. Sally Harper, whose AHRC-funded project *The Experience of Worship in Late Medieval Cathedral and Parish Church*, at Bangor University, was the source of much valuable reflection. A conversation with Mike Riley was the starting-point for the present exploration. For astute guidance and swift passage through the Press I thank Hans Christoffersen, Lauren Murphy, Colleen Stiller, and Patrick McGowan.

Dr. Daniel Grimley and the Rev. Dr. Jonathan Arnold have been patient and supportive colleagues in many ways. My wife, Dr. Jennifer Rushworth, in addition to serving as Italian translator, has helped untiringly in many more ways—editorial, critical, and domestic—to bring this work to completion, and deserves a proper holiday.

Oxford
St. Jerome, 2013

Introduction

Lex orandi, lex credendi
The law of prayer is the law of belief.

The title of this book draws upon the first verse of Psalm 64: "Hear my voice, O God, in my prayer." It establishes clearly the axiom that worship and prayer are addressed to God. The imperative mood identifies the action desired on God's part, and it suggests that the human mind has ways of expressing itself which are appropriate and comprehensible to its Divine Author. This is a complicated undertaking. There have been countless efforts to express how and why human attempts to address the transcendent succeed or fail. St. Augustine (d. 430), trying to establish some of the parameters, writes thus about the nature of hymns, from which we may derive an approach to the organized worship of the church more generally.

> Do you know what a hymn is? It is a song in praise of God. If you praise God without singing, you are not offering a hymn. If you sing but do not praise God, that is not a hymn either. If you praise something else, something unconnected with the praise of God, then, even though you are singing praise, you are not singing a hymn. A hymn implies three things: it must be sung, it must consist of praise, and the praise must be offered to God. The praise of God, when sung, is called a hymn.[1]

Augustine's unequivocal definition may seem overly legalistic, but it is lucid, and it assumes that praise sung to a transcendent God is effective. By contrast, Ludwig Wittgenstein (d. 1951) held that the transcendent and the mystical were in fact inaccessible through

[1] *The Works of Saint Augustine: A Translation for the Twenty-First Century, vol. III/20, Expositions on the Psalms 121–150*, ed. Boniface Ramsey, trans. Maria Boulding (New York: New City Press, 2004), 490.

language and human expression: the limits of language, he argued in his *Tractatus Logico-Philosophicus*, were the limits of the world.[2] Anything addressed beyond the world was inexpressible.

Wittgenstein's proposition is evidently not understood to be the case by those who employ human language to praise and pray to a deity: language in this case is an opportunity for intersection between human experience and divine totality. Worship challenges the boundaries between the world and the transcendent. It also gives rise to the aphorism given above, *lex orandi, lex credendi:* the law of prayer [is] the law of belief. Christians understand that the teaching of the church is clearly presented in a special way in their forms of worship, and that worship is the unique, privileged means through which the church and its many members enter into a dialogue with God.

Aside from the second part of this introduction, which considers the concept and practice of worship in the present day, this book is about a time when the vast majority of people in the West were Christians, and when the vast majority of Christians went to church. Why the church itself should exist is a related question to the establishment of the function of worship, because the point of the church, at least as it was understood until quite recently in the popular imagination, has not been to be one of a host of charitable organizations doing good in the world, or to help individuals explore their own relationship with the divine: in fact, the point of the church was to offer collective praise and thanksgiving to God. If this book's title seems surprisingly individualistic, recall that many of the texts of the psalms are expressed in the first person (for instance: "I will give thanks to the Lord with my whole heart" [Ps 9:1]), and that interiorized faith, throughout history, was often articulated through such forms.

Worship accepts (following our title) that God can *hear* the voices of the faithful, including one's own *individual* voice, and that God necessarily exists. This is not a book about the sociological functions of religion; rather, it is about (and tries to depict through several historical episodes) the life of the church and how liturgy

[2] Ludwig Wittgenstein, *Tractatus Logico-Philosophicus*, proposition 5.6 (London: Routledge Classics, 2001), 68.

has functioned within the beliefs, doctrines, and practices of a people of faith. It is not about the mechanics of the precise forms of worship which have been observed; rather, it is about interrelationships between form and function, which will prove especially interesting when either form or function may change.

THE PURPOSE OF THIS BOOK

Faced with a world in which the worship of the past and present continues to resonate deeply, it is the aim of this book to enable students of a wide range of disciplines, together with those who have an interest in the history of the Christian church, to consider in particular the *functional dimensions* of worship, meaning the hermeneutic or significative functions or, more simply, what Christian worship has *meant* to its contemporaries across the centuries.

This task seems at first rather unnecessary, for it may be obvious in any given scenario what worship may have meant: its role should be clear from its cultural context and, more fundamentally, from what we can extract from our personal experience and knowledge of the church, liturgy, music, and culture. Yet even (and perhaps especially) within an intentionally Christian context, there is a tendency to assume that we know and understand the rationale, the motivations, and the understandings that buttress the liturgical practices of Christians of all epochs, because it is all too easy to equate present-day practice with that of any other historical period, and thereby equate a known and comprehensible scenario with one that is less well understood, which has perhaps emerged from another culture, churchmanship, or theology. This is not at all an unusual situation, because most human activity is remarked upon and framed within an existing realm of experience. But to try to pigeonhole in this way some historical act of worship—for instance the baptism of an infant—into our own limited realm of experience, even if we have experienced many infant baptisms in our own age, is to mistake the proverbial cuckoo's egg as one of our own brood. Christian worship, despite its apparent similarity of form from age to age (another illusion!), has in fact undergone many changes in respect of its function.

It is perhaps forgivable that misconceptions about the unbroken continuity of the signification of worship rites should occur.

Worship, by its very definition, is symbolic and expressive of wider truths which are implied or conveyed by acts of memory and repetition, whether these be from Scripture (the universal constant in Christian worship) or part of the very extensive extrascriptural network of liturgical text, music, movement, and symbol, including hymns and songs as well as other texts in the liturgical tradition, some of which have their roots in the earliest written evidence of Christian worship, others in successive movements and documents.

Worship illustrates doctrine, but it also helps to influence it. Yet as I have argued, we have a tendency to understand symbols in ways which we already comprehend, which is one of the reasons for misunderstanding. It is true that Christian worship is enacted to and for "the greater glory of God," but to be satisfied with such a definition alone is to underestimate vastly its significance both mystically, spiritually, and culturally.

This volume is neither a history of Christian worship nor an explanation of the niceties of ceremonial. Nor is it a survey of the habits of some particular worship tradition. Books on liturgical topics tend typically to be divisible into two categories: those dealing with historical and philological matters (pitched mainly at academic specialists); and those with a pastoral dimension (generally associated with "liturgy" or "liturgics" as an applied discipline in ministerial formation or continuing education). Rarely do these specialized, challenging approaches suit the needs of readers who are not seeking an in-depth analysis of the mechanics or theology of worship. The present volume, by contrast, seeks to diminish the distance between these methods, exploring both aspects. It seeks, rather, to engage with the cultural and intellectual context of worship which serves as a middle ground. It is a guide for students and other non-specialist readers to the changing *functions* of Christian worship in historical perspective (What does worship *do*? What is its purpose?), an important element whose wider understanding is fraught with often indefensible stereotypes that are rarely challenged. For instance, the "Eucharist" as a concept in the year 2013 usually takes a form essentially similar to the one used in the year 1313, but the pluralistic conceptions of the rite (anything from the reenactment of a simple shared meal to a solemn High Mass in which the divine is literally made present) and all the potential cultural functions these conceptions imply in the twenty-first century would be almost unrecognizable to a fourteenth-century Christian. "Active participation," as conceived in the present day, is a very new concept, previously unheard of in Christian history except at its inception.

It is all too clear that this short volume cannot hope to explain in any depth the contemporary significance of the multitude of rites of worship, not least because the fullest such explanations need to come from specialists in the arcane knowledge of each period. I focus, then, on the development and practice of daily public prayer, and on the Eucharist, necessarily branching away from these central rites where other elements demand attention. The chapters of this book are episodic and incomplete by nature, arranged in reverse chronological order to avoid teleological conclusions on the part of author or reader. Each chapter focuses on a few developments in order to draw out both the unique features of a historical period and to allow a particular scenario to be discussed in depth. It is, therefore, a study in historical perspective, a series of scenes from a wider happening. But it is not a comprehensive history. It focuses on expressions of Western Christianity, leaving (for the most part) antecedent Jewish forms and the unique perspective of the Eastern churches to more qualified hands.

Some conclusions, though, are constant. In the most general sense, this book will argue that while worship has always been a central activity of Christian life, its pragmatic functions have changed substantially, a point which is often missed in favor of oversimplification of the purpose of worship. Examples are legion: early Christian worship had the veiled effect of bringing a persecuted minority community together; the medieval Mass allowed for a surprising degree of personal devotion, but also nonverbal participation from the laity, bringing them into a wider communion with the rest of the praying church, the body of Christ; nineteenth-century ecclesiologists saw in the restoration of the grand ceremony, music, and decoration of the medieval church an opportunity to recapture in their own time the fervent piety of the Middle Ages. The title of the book emphasizes the independent and colorful voices of each community studied, the particular significance of individual experience, the stress on "functional" dimensions highlights the fact that in all cases worship is performative, that is, that its performance "does something," one element of worship that is a constant.

It will be helpful to consider the connections between the *form* of worship and its *function*. Broadly speaking, the form of a rite normally corresponds to its function: for instance, the texts and actions involved in baptism are representative of the (implied) cleansing and washing spiritual function of the rite. Sometimes, without the function apparently changing, a form may be expanded or amended, although never contrary to its purpose. This change happens often through the extension or embellishment ("troping") of a text or melody, or through increased complexity of the undertaking, as in the appearance of processions in the later Middle Ages. It is primarily with changes in the function of the rite that substantial changes are made to the form. An innovation in form may appear, for instance, when the function of a rite demands that a lay audience be able to understand it, or to be instructed in their faith by it, a principle which was the motivator for the widespread use of vernacular language by sixteenth-century reformers and equally by mid-twentieth-century developments in the Roman Catholic Church. In the Middle Ages the reception of consecrated bread and wine at the Eucharist by the celebrating priest alone was a consequence of the principal lay obligation of *being present* at the sacrifice. Where possible in subsequent chapters the relationship between form and function will be underlined.

"Liturgy" and "worship" are both terms that have been defined in many different ways, sometimes at cross-purposes. It is worth discussing what they mean in the context of this book. "Worship" is derived from the Old English *weorðscipe*, worth-ship, a word that encompasses both the act and the worthiness of the recipient. What is worth worshipping, and how worship is done, are inexhaustibly variable: in the words of twenty-first-century spiritual director Rachelle Mee-Chapman, "In emerging churches, all things are worship: everyday conversation or watching kids skateboard and seeing their devotion to practice, passion, and skills."[3]

[3] Eddie Gibbs and Ryan Bolger, *Emerging Churches: Creating Christian Community in Postmodern Cultures* (London: SPCK, 2006), 222.

"Liturgy" has its origin in the Greek word *leitourgia*, meaning the "work of the people," with an emphasis on the corporate nature of the activity. It has come, however, to be associated particularly with the organized and regulated rites by which worship is enacted, sometimes even to the celebration of the Eucharist alone (i.e., the "Divine Liturgy"). The so-called "liturgical" churches (broadly speaking Roman Catholics, Anglicans, Lutherans, and others who follow fixed, historically guided forms in their public activities) are sometimes distinguished from the "nonliturgical," i.e., those whose worship takes a freer or extemporized form. I would argue that this separation is not helpful. It gives rise to an artificial distinction between forms that are fixed and others that are not. In my view, "liturgy" and "worship" are broadly synonymous, as in John Harper's definition: "liturgy embraces all the formal worship of a corporate Christian community."[4] Indeed, even among Christians who have sought to move away from tradition and precedent, the term "liturgy," particularly with its inclusive etymology, is sometimes rehabilitated: emerging church leader Sue Wallace writes, "Liturgy and ritual do not have to be dirty words. They can be rediscovered, and if they are relevant and meaningful, they can be amazingly powerful."[5]

✣ ✣ ✣

This book's constituent chapters, each of which treats a different episode in the history of the Christian church, will raise the following questions:

1. Why did Christians go to church? *Why worship?*
2. *What happened* to them there, substantively and otherwise, and how did they respond?

With these particular queries, as well as passages from contemporaneous theological and liturgical texts as a starting-point, the

[4] John Harper, *The Forms and Orders of Western Liturgy from the Tenth to the Eighteenth Century: A Historical Introduction and Guide for Students and Musicians* (Oxford, UK: Clarendon Press, 1991), 12.

[5] Gibbs and Bolger, *Emerging Churches*, 224.

reader will be encouraged to consider carefully the evidence for the functions of Christian worship.

"SPIRITUALITY," MEGACHURCHES, AND THE "REFORM OF THE REFORM": FUNCTIONS OF WORSHIP TODAY

The 2011 census in the United Kingdom suggests that just over ten percent of the population attend weekly church services, and a further twenty-five percent attend church at least once a year, apart from services such as baptisms, weddings, and funerals. The increasingly multicultural face of Britain means that Christian beliefs have been joined by those of many other theistic religions, especially Islam, whose adherents make up five percent of the population.[6] Over a quarter of adults surveyed in 2007, of whom a slightly larger proportion were women, believed in "something," but they were not sure what that "something" was.[7] Church attendance in the United States is considerably higher, but regular worshippers are still a minority. In both countries, broadly described as Christian at least in heritage (59.3% of residents in the United Kingdom identify as Christian[8]), fewer people than ever before have any substantive knowledge of the Bible, Christian ideas or doctrines, or familiarity with organized worship, other than in its broadest objectives.

This state of affairs is precipitated by not only a disenfranchisement with the church on the part of formerly practicing Christians, but also the fact that as older generations die out, fewer and fewer people have had even infrequent exposure to Christian worship.

[6] "Full Story: What Does the Census Tell Us about Religion in 2011?" Office of National Statistics, report, May 16, 2013, http://www.ons.gov.uk/ons/dcp171776_310454.pdf. Accessed November 15, 2013.

[7] Office of National Statistics, *Social Trends 40: Lifestyles and Social Participation,* http://www.ons.gov.uk/ons/rel/social-trends-rd/social-trends/social-trends-40/social-trends-40—lifestyles-and-social-participation-chapter.pdf. Sixteen percent of adults surveyed agreed with the statement "I am an atheist. The whole notion of a supernatural god is nonsense."

[8] "Percentage of the population with no religion has increased in England and Wales," Office of National Statistics website, http://www.ons.gov.uk/ons/rel/census/2011-census/key-statistics-for-local-authorities-in-england-and-wales/sty-religion.html. Accessed November 11, 2013.

British surveys suggest that about 40 percent nationwide are "unchurched," meaning that they have never attended church, even occasionally. This figure increases, up to 80 percent, in urban areas.[9]

The controversial and enigmatic utterance "God is dead," issued by Friedrich Nietzsche in the late nineteenth century and further explored as a symbol of the growth of atheism throughout the twentieth, finds considerable support and confirmation in the fact that it is possible for someone in Western civilization (formerly termed "the Christian West") to live a complete life, never having made a conscious choice to do so, with no need or desire to interact with religion (organized or otherwise) or with the transcendent. Civil weddings and secular funerals are uncontroversial and fulfilling replacements for their religious alternatives. Increasing burdens on time mean that Sunday, traditionally the day set aside for corporate Christian worship, is also in demand for family and community activities, and the "Victorian" observance of the Sabbath, restricting activities in favor of hallowing the day, is viewed as unreasonably strict. The ban on transacting business, until relatively recently upheld in part by Sunday shopping laws, has been lifted in many places.[10]

Despite the fact that Christianity retains some cultural and historical significance in the pluralistic, postmodern West, the diminishing congregations attending organized church services after a historically recognizable pattern appear to show that there is a decreasing appetite for worship of this sort and also, more generally, for organized religion. Worship might be seen as unnecessary, an opportunity for those with strong doctrinal views to proselytize, and to be intolerant of individualistic belief systems. It is also worth mentioning that in most Western civilizations, it is culturally acceptable and indeed sometimes desirable *not* to be a Christian. Aside from a sense of postcolonial shame over the "civilizing" influence

[9] *Mission-Shaped Church: Church Planting and Fresh Expressions of Church in a Changing Context*, ed. Mission and Public Affairs Council, Church of England, 2nd ed. (London: Church House Publishing, 2009), 37.

[10] In the UK (2013), while shops with floor-space less than 280 square meters may open at any hour of any day of the week, shops larger than this size may only open for six hours between 10 a.m. and 6 p.m.

of Christian practice in mission lands, the postmodern critique of institutions, doctrines, and systems, together with a florescence of alternative cultural practices that satisfy the community-cohesion and existential functions of religion, mean that the perceived top-down approach and endemic corruption of an institution that has outlived its time seem to outweigh any potential spiritual benefits. Present-day criticisms are legion for a church that despite its perceived high moral standpoint, fixed codes of behavior, and self-identification with minorities and the oppressed, is apparently depersonalized, sexist, intolerant, and dominated by a strong, wealthy, powerful hierarchy. Secular society, by contrast, appears to encourage a radically inclusive, open-minded approach that is not narrow minded enough even to suggest there may be one ideal belief system. Because for practicing Christians and outside observers alike, the church is identified with and is most obviously manifest in its public acts of worship, a similar judgment is passed on the services of the church which may appear to be an incredible amount of time spent worshipping an invisible, nonimmanent deity, propounding a strong moral message, and excluding outsiders while also being framed with archaic language, historically dubious texts, and esoteric symbolism. Thus worship traditions associated with unpopular doctrinal positions are written off along with the perceived intolerance and inflexibility of their practitioners.

Perhaps because the expected pattern of traditional Sunday worship is associated with a high level of doctrinal control and fixity, interest in internalized searches for the transcendent (explorations which often identify with the term "spirituality" rather than "religion") is catered to by many new forms of service within traditional and less traditional frameworks that are designed to introduce "seekers" to the Christian faith, as well as in new forms of Christian gathering that aim to bring together believers and seekers alike who have other common interests, for instance nightclub culture or a place of business. It is also the force behind the outpouring of interest in alternative forms of "spirituality" outside organized religion. An almost unimaginable variety of forms of enquiry (and worship) have emerged, in part perhaps because the element of seemingly limitless choice is one of the ever-present principles of present-day living, and in part because people's reasons for going to church may differ in as many ways as exist styles of worship. This profusion of choice makes it difficult for us to conceptualize why anyone in the past, let alone all Western Christians, would have bothered to adhere to such an inflexible obligation, even if a concern with the practice of worship or to historical forms of liturgical text, music, action, or theology is often in the remit of those who are concerned with related forms of cultural activity.

It is with the somewhat pessimistic scenario presented earlier in this introduction that we begin to explore the functionality of worship through a brief look at the present day.

Why worship? Responding to the first of our principal questions posed in the case of the former "Christian West," we must recognize that a very large proportion of the population do not attend church, and in fact many of the two billion people who identify as "Christian" are not in the habit of attending public worship on a regular basis. But this is a result of the sentiment behind the real answer to the question: never before the twentieth century have Christians "gone to church," or *not* gone to church, for as many different reasons, influenced by as many different strands of spirituality identifying as Christian, employing as many disparate forms of public worship as can be imagined. Because to be Christian is broadly but completely defined as being a follower of Jesus Christ, whether this allegiance falls within the remit of any of the enormous range of organized subcategories of institutional Christianity appears to be immaterial, as does the traditional imperative to attend some form of worship in community, no matter how much liturgical theologians insist that corporate gatherings are the authentic expression of the body of Christ, the church. For perhaps the first time, it is possible to identify as a Christian without an allegiance to one or another organized form of worship.

The second of the principal questions may be answered for the present day in as many ways as the first. *What happens in church?* It follows that in addition to the wide variety of mainline denominational styles of worship, many of which have existed historically, there exist a very large number of styles of Christian community gathering which give the impression and effect of ritualized worship, while not avowedly subscribing to the idea that a repeatable, organized event, however extemporized in execution, can or should be equated with "ritual" of any sort. Never has there been a wider range of worship styles, but many can be associated readily with the priorities which have existed throughout Christian history: the glorification and praise-giving to a merciful God, the sharing of word and sacrament, and the building up of a community descended from the disciples of Christ.

It is also worth mentioning that the state of present-day Christianity resembles, in several ways, that of the disciples of Christ who celebrated the rites of the nascent church in the years before the Christian religion became legal in AD 313, the "Peace of Constantine." It is certainly true that practicing, confessing Christians, like their counterparts 1700 years ago, are in a small minority and sometimes discouraged by external parties from practicing their faith. There can be a "high social cost" (as opposed to a threat to life) that discourages Christians from exercising, for instance, the public ministry of evangelism. It is also worth mentioning that in many forms of church, small group/cell group ministry, similar to the small-scale meetings of the persecuted church in members' houses, are popular, and the meal-sharing of the Alpha Course, also sometimes held in private homes, could be said to resemble the shared meals of the earliest Christian communities.

The failure of forms of worship to be explicable, relevant, or appealing to consumers of religion and spirituality leads Eddie Gibbs and Ryan Bolger, authors of a study of "emerging churches," to describe a situation where "the majority of current church practices are cultural accommodations to a society that no longer exists."[11] Similarly Paul Heelas and Linda Woodhead, in *The Spiritual Revolution: Why Religion Is Giving Way to Spirituality*, write that the "great historical bond between Western cultures and a Christianity whose characteristic mode is to make appeal to transcendent authority is dissolving."[12] The Church of England's document *Mission-Shaped*

[11] Gibbs and Bolger, *Emerging Churches*, 19.

[12] Paul Heelas et al., *The Spiritual Revolution: Why Religion Is Giving Way to Spirituality* (Oxford, UK: Blackwell, 2005), 10.

Church makes very clear that in its own heartland, Christianity is "in a critical missionary situation."[13] Yet in the face of this apparently resolute rejection of *organized* religion, many people continue to aspire to a relationship with the transcendent.

Although a sense of disenfranchisement with church institutions, including worship services, has been widely associated with the later twentieth century, as early as 1906 the liturgical scholar and Anglican religious Walter Howard Frere recognized that many people who liked ceremonies and rituals in some places tended to despise them in a church context, an observation which in the early twentieth century was linked most closely to disputes over churchmanship (particular stances on doctrines and practices) in the Church of England, an institution which since its foundation has been forced to contend with great variety in both doctrine and liturgical practices, the former often in a complicated relationship with the latter. "Ceremonial is at one moment the outcome of doctrine," wrote Frere, "and at another the inculcator of it, at another a perverter of it."[14] It may be this very close association to doctrine, another element that is fixed, that diminishes the attraction of organized worship, particularly when forms of service deliberately underline the central precepts of faith, for instance in the recitation of one of the Creeds, the foundational professions of faith, by clergy and congregation, or even in the collective singing of hymns. By its very definition, liturgy helps to inculcate and give expression to belief, and the practice of ritual without the associated sentiment is next to meaningless. Yet there is a strong attraction to formulating and practicing habits and ritual actions, and this tendency, linked with the materialistic, tangible nature of human experience, as well as the appeal of the transcendent, means that the search for the spiritual can be manifested in different material ways.[15]

[13] *Mission-Shaped Church*, 12.

[14] Walter Howard Frere, *The Principles of Religious Ceremonial*, 2nd ed. (London: A.R. Mowbray, 1928), 10.

[15] See Austin Farrer, *The Glass of Vision* (London: Dacre Press, 1948), and John Macquarrie, *A Guide to the Sacraments* (London: SCM Press, 1997).

One expression of human spirituality particularly prevalent at the present time is found in the phrase "spiritual and not religious." But what does this mean? To have a hankering for the transcendent without being a confessing member of an organized body? Or to accept Jesus or some other manifestation of a deity as a teacher/moral guide? Or merely to embrace the obscure, profound, mysterious aspects of inward faith? Or to be safely relativistic and say that all religions are one/equally valid? Or does it mean that the speaker would rather not rule the option out? It is difficult to define this phrase because it, like other post-positivist concepts, escapes a single definition. Is it just a "turn of phrase" rather than an identity? (In succeeding chapters dealing with periods before the twentieth century, "spirituality" will refer not to this modern phenomenon but to the wider Christian spiritual enterprise.)

The pervasive and influential postmodern critique which emerged in the late twentieth century, described by Jean-François Lyotard as "incredulity towards metanarratives" or, put more simply, a devaluing of systems, teleologies, and the modernist dialectic of the earlier part of the century, has exerted a predictably chaotic influence on fixed forms of worship. It is a product of the postmodern experience that choice, and plurality, are prioritized because metanarratives which supply a clear prerogative to a single course of action have been rejected. Given that up to eighty percent of the population is "unchurched," that is, with no present or prior Christian ecclesial identity or experience, people who are seeking spiritual experience are in a position where they need to "shop" for religious experiences that suit them, an extended analogy put forward by Bryan Spinks in his book *The Worship Mall*. Not only must they choose the Christian religion (whatever that may mean), it is now necessary to choose from a wide and potentially bewildering array of worship styles, organized denominations, demographically defined church groups, and spiritualities in a way that Christians of an earlier period, even those from the times of reform, would have found surprisingly subjective and individualistic.

Some mainstream churches have recognized the need for "inculturation," or the adaptation of Christian rites to align with existing cultural norms, not only in the case of the developing world, where Western conventions may not be suitable expressions for communities with very different worldviews,[16] but also in their customary environments, where, in the words of the York Statement, *"Down to Earth" Worship*, issued by a group of Anglican clergy and scholars in 1989, "a lack of inculturation has fostered both the cultural alienation of some Christians and an over-ready willingness of others to live in two different cultures, one of their religion and the other of their daily life."[17] This observation very clearly identifies a critical issue, one which has occupied most of the designers of the new patterns for worship which have emerged in the last fifty years or so: that the language, or the style, or the music, or the physical appearance of worship (both in the Western world and outside) bear very little resemblance to any equivalents in the secular world. For some this is not an issue, as the material and the transcendent necessarily take different forms (the often-mocked archaism of language identified with the King James Bible and the Book of Common Prayer has also been described as a special linguistic way of identifying the sacred) but for others it poses a real problem for inclusivity, and the "worship mall" includes a vast range of options for shoehorning religion into different cultural environments.

One of the most prevalent and successful options "shoppers" have, and one which corresponds reasonably well to previous incarnations of church, but which embraces the habits and preferences of the twenty-first-century faith environment is the so-called *megachurch*, defined by Spinks as a Protestant church averaging 2,000 attendees in weekend services.[18] Megachurches often craft "seekers' services" on Sundays. These services are accessible to

[16] For the Roman Catholic Church in particular, see the works of Anscar Chupungco, i.e., *Liturgies of the Future: The Process and Methods of Inculturation* (New York: Paulist Press, 1989).

[17] In David Holeton, ed., *Liturgical Inculturation in the Anglican Communion, Including the York Statement "Down to Earth" Worship* (Cambridge, UK: Grove Books Ltd., 1990), 15:9.

[18] Bryan Spinks, *The Worship Mall: Contemporary Responses to Christian Culture* (London: SPCK, 2010), 63.

outsiders and are designed for their needs. They are often the church's primary offering. In this scenario, worship serves as a means of introducing the Christian story to people with little experience of church. Timothy Wright, of the Community of Grace, Arizona, in the United States, writes that seekers' services must be well signposted both literally and in the service sheet, prioritizing "presentation over participation, celebration over the cerebral, and intimacy over awe," allowing those who are less familiar with the practices of worship as well as the basic principles of Christianity to be clearly presented.[19]

Music is often used to make those unfamiliar with the form of the service comfortable, to allow them to sit back and enjoy rather than participate actively, and visitors are welcomed warmly and presented with information about the church to take home: if a collection is taken, often visitors are told not to contribute but to supply their contact details instead, so that the church can contact them personally.

The Church of England's document *Mission-Shaped Church* highlights very clearly that even geography, irrespective of spirituality, is no longer a major determinant of congregational identity. Communities, it says, are now built around "leisure, work, and friendship," and consequently, "the gospel has to meet people where they are."[20] The adoption of a religion, and the choice of that religion, is an open choice in a quasi-consumerist scenario where the idea of free choice is central, particularly when identification as a committed Christian seems more important. Similarly, the writers of *Mission-Shaped Church* believe that the missionary scenario of the Church of England, together with the responsibility of that body, is to be an all-encompassing, national church. This means that fresh expressions of church—for instance, worship or prayer meetings centered around a school, place of work, or shared interest—may be more suitable to the reception of new worshippers than a traditional "congregation."[21] Yet for some there are clear disadvantages

[19] Ibid., 81.

[20] *Mission-Shaped Church*, 6.

[21] Ibid., 23.

in expressions of "church" that do not involve a building or a Sunday service also called "church": as Gibbs and Bolger write, "the desire for church to be a meeting at a particular place and time is hard to shake," and without these components the service, however committed, seems to lacks legitimacy. Equally critics wonder whether "fresh expressions" are capable of being sustained by Christian communities which also need to serve their existing congregations: if existing forms of worship appear to "work," there is little motivation or incentive to change.

"Blended" or alternative worship incorporates elements from a variety of sources to suit particular circumstances, and is associated with the pastiche culture of postmodernity. Here worship embraces plurality, doubt, nonbelief, and nontraditional churchgoing through stimuli familiar from the wider world or from art and music. Gibbs and Bolger separate such forms from the megachurch and "young adult services" targeted at the "millennial" generation, which are described as repackaged forms of traditional church.[22] Jonny Baker, one of the leaders of Grace, an alternative congregation in London, appropriates the idea of "curation" from the art world as an alternative to "leading worship." Curators of worship can be, he says, "midwives, DJs, brokers, fools, middlewomen, encouragers, magpies."[23] The idea at the heart of alternative worship is to take "a vulgar, secular space and change it in some way."[24] There are many similarities between the external form of traditional worship and the stimulus of art and music in these experimental forms of curated worship, not so much in their appearance but in the way that they are apprehended by the participant. "You have a sacramental theology," writes Baker, "making connections between the presence of God and very ordinary day-to-day stuff. I really love that, particularly as often worship can seem so divorced from everyday life experience."[25] Similarly Nic Hughes, one of the founders of the British church Vaux, writes, "Christianity provided

[22] Gibbs and Bolger, *Emerging Churches,* 45.

[23] Jonny Baker, *Curating Worship* (London: SPCK, 2010), 9.

[24] Baker, xiii, 24.

[25] Baker, 141.

the exo-skeleton, both physically and conceptually. It became a resource, a vast playground to re-pattern faith."[26] Spinks supplies some further examples of "blended" worship: the "U2charist," which features the music, full of Scriptural references, of the well-known band; the "Duke Ellington Mass"; and the "Hip-hop Eucharist," which applies the vocabulary of hip-hop culture to the celebration; as well as the liturgy of St. Gregory of Nyssa, San Francisco, a church which has adopted artistic elements from a wide range of world cultures and refashioned liturgies into new but recognizable forms.[27]

In the millennial Roman Catholic Church, with the election of Pope Benedict XVI came a series of liturgical developments popularly known as "the reform of the reform," a reference to the very considerable changes initiated by the Second Vatican Council and, forty years later, seen as ripe for further revision and clarification. Pope Benedict eased restrictions on the use of the pre-Vatican II order of service for the Mass, strongly encouraged the cultivation of skill in the traditional plainchant of the church and, most noticeably, endorsed the retranslation into the vernacular of the authorized Latin edition of the liturgy, meaning that Catholics who had been celebrating Mass with the same texts since they were first translated after the council were asked to learn and embrace new translations seen by some as more faithful to the Latin, less reductive, and generally richer in imagery, allusion, and style.

There is a noticeable similarity in both the emerging churches and in churches which normally adhere to the ecclesial conventions of earlier times, namely to find alternatives to forms of worship that make assumptions about the pre-existent belief of the people who attend. Worship, like all church activity, is seen as necessarily missional, bringing both the Gospel and the present-day practices of the church into the open.

Many Christian writers have contemplated the association of material things with the divine, and seeing and hearing remarkable things (for instance perhaps, the description of the New Jerusalem

[26] Quoted in Baker, 100.

[27] Spinks, 5–6.

in the Revelation of St. John) can be associated in Scripture with the idea of beauty. Beauty in the material world can also be equated with divine beauty, the complex things in creation viewed in conjunction with unknowable divine truths that are simultaneously too complex and simple to be comprehended in any other way. Light and beauty are synonyms for the divine, as in the Creed: God from God, Light from Light. In the same way if God is unknowable, he is reflected in things that can be known. A critical example of this is the manifestation of God in Christ, God made man, manifest in the Eucharist and in the proclaimed Word. God may also be seen in the beautiful things of creation which, when helping to form the fullness of the liturgy, also point out and reflect the Creator of all things, praising him for his goodness and celebrating all that God's people have been given, from everyday conversation and watching skateboards to the grace received in the sacraments. This interpretation of liturgical function may hold true in the present-day world, but it has also been true from age to age in varied and exciting ways, as the subsequent chapters will illustrate.

Chapter 1 explores the roles played by the liturgy in the interactions between the church and the modern world, particularly through the lens of the Second Vatican Council and of the liturgical reforms of the twentieth century in the Anglican Communion. Central to this vision is the realization of "full and active participation" of the laity in liturgical worship. In chapter 2, the groundwork for this participation is seen in the Liturgical Movement and the Romantic ideals behind the restoration of historic practices, particularly in the restoration of plainchant and medieval ceremonial, as well as the reprioritization of the sacraments within the life of the worshipping church. Chapter 3 considers the effects of changing theological emphases, both Catholic and Protestant, on the worship of the Western church as for the first time it was divided. Liturgy became a means of expressing the faith of a congregation, as well as building it up through exegesis. In Chapter 4, worship is seen as the single most important occupation of the church, the focus of clerical and lay religious life, and a source of aesthetic inspiration in the later Middle Ages. The interiorization of devotion in this period meant that the liturgy served as the setting for personal acts of piety. Chapter 5 considers the implications of the legal and official status of Christianity, including the development of large-scale institutions (monasteries) built around a schedule of worship. Chapter 6 returns to the scriptural and patristic record to examine later claims of authenticity and divine institution for the sacraments and other worship of the church. In each of these episodes of Christian history, the forms, settings, and theology of worship will be introduced, and their varied functions explored.

CHAPTER 1

"Full and Active Participation"

> *Mother Church earnestly desires that all the faithful should be led to that fully conscious and active participation in liturgical celebrations which is demanded by the very nature of the liturgy.*
>
> —Sacrosanctum Concilium, II.14

Imagine entering a Sunday service of the twentieth or twenty-first century taking place in a Catholic church or in one of the mainline Protestant churches. It is quite likely that your imagined service, whatever your own experience of church may be (or may not be), will involve some dialogue between the presider and the congregation (and, perhaps more obviously, that there will be a congregation), as well as some other opportunities to contribute to the service, possibly through singing hymns, and almost certainly through the reading of the Bible. This familiar (or less familiar) scenario is, quite predictably, based on the assumptions that the congregation should be made to feel included, that inclusion mainly comes from verbally participating or being verbally addressed, and that attending the service will help the congregation to grow in their own faith through the sharing of the good news of Christ, through the dialogue and the ritual, and perhaps through the sharing of bread and wine. Yet these assumptions about what constitutes "participation," and particularly "full and active participation" date back, in terms of their impact on worship, only to the middle part of the twentieth century, when, despite outwardly presenting a face of continuity, the Christian church dramatically changed the presentation of its worship with a wide range of follow-on effects.

At first glance, the period in question does not appear to be one that was ripe for reform. The spectacular changes in the worshipping practices of the several Christian churches around the time of the European Reformations, as they went their separate ways, can be seen to have been an inevitable result of deep-seated theological and social change. It might be more surprising that similarly dramatic change—in both the forms of worship and their influence on Christian people—took place in the twentieth century, a time of comparatively little religious upheaval and dwindling religious practice, after over three hundred years of relative fixity in which Roman Catholics, Anglicans, and Lutherans (being the main "liturgical" churches) had settled into reasonably established forms, some of which (the Roman Catholic Mass, for instance, and nearly all of the Book of Common Prayer of the Church of England) remained in the precise form they had had at their inception.[1] Yet it was precisely the settled nature of worship that stimulated an ecumenical council of the Catholic Church whose first priority was a reseating of the liturgy within the paradigm of the modern world.

Here it is worth recalling the balancing act between form and function presented in the introduction. Though prescribed forms of worship had remained relatively fixed, the same could not necessarily be said for their desired function, particularly in a changed world where levels of literacy, education, and religious instruction were dramatically different than three hundred years previous. Among many other influences, forms of communication, emerging art forms, worldwide travel, and changed living habits significantly altered the way that people, including Christians, were interacting with the world around them. The intellectual world had been shaken by the effects of the Enlightenment, when the value of long-held ideals and the methodology of scholarship came into question, and no assumption was safe from doubt, thanks to the inception of "natural philosophy" (the original name for science) and the social acceptability of skepticism. In the early twentieth

[1] More or less unrelated developments (except as a means of contrast) were taking place in the Reformed and Free Churches which, in trying to come to terms with their function and doctrine, were continuously developing new forms of worship.

century, two world wars had forced society to consider seriously its morals. Worship was the public and accessible face of a religion whose mysteries were still opaque to the laity, but control of its forms was important to ecclesiastical authorities and also consequently an area for experimentation and political statement, for instance during the English Protectorate and in nineteenth-century France.[2]

This discontinuity between form and function did not go unnoticed by contemporary commentators. In the early days of the twentieth century, the noted liturgical scholar (and architect *manqué* of Anglican worship) Walter Howard Frere, variously Anglican Bishop of Truro and founding member of the religious order of the Community of the Resurrection, proposed a three-part cycle of liturgical development which he believed could encapsulate and explain, as well as perhaps predict, the storied development of liturgy throughout Christian history. At the beginning of the cycle, patterns of worship went through a stage of experiment and innovation. In the second part, established forms experienced consolidation and settlement. The final stage was a period of stagnation and decay.

Writing in 1906, Frere believed that the church was in the third of these stages, with liturgy no longer suitable to purpose. He believed that some of the admirable functions of worship for the faithful, such as edification and the inspiration of awe, were insufficiently exploited, in part because of the inappropriateness of the archaic forms in use and the improvised modifications to them. The present-day theologian John Macquarrie has echoed these sentiments, writing that rituals quite predictably have a tendency "to become more elaborate," but that such accretions can harm the overall effect of the rite (an opinion shared by the medieval writer Thomas Aquinas, explored in chapter 5). Macquarrie writes that sometimes, "words and ceremonial . . . of the sacraments need to be revised and even drastically cut back."[3]

[2] See Katharine Ellis, *The Politics of Plainchant in fin-de-siècle France* (Farnham, UK: Ashgate, 2013).

[3] Macquarrie, *A Guide to the Sacraments*, 63.

In the mid-twentieth century, in fact, encouraging active participation necessitated putting, for the first time, many of the words of the liturgy in the mouths of the faithful. The Tridentine Low Mass,[4] because the text could be spoken entirely by the celebrant, appeared to carry no participative value for the hearer, even if it was beautifully written and full of devotional language.

In the face of diminishing adherence to religion and criticisms of ecclesiastical authority, as well as the enormous growth of alternative forms in the wide range of new churches designed to suit every taste and requirement, churches of the 1960s were using forms of worship not really updated since their inception. They faced a changing theological consensus about the operation of worship within the life of the church and the agency of the individual. These problems were compounded by the continuing threats of atheism and scientific rationality.

The twentieth-century state of affairs owed much to the Liturgical Movement (discussed more fully in chapter 2), a pan-Western series of influences which strove to return worship to a place of centrality in the activities of Christians, to prioritize the celebration of the Eucharist above devotional practices, and to inspire deep personal spirituality. The consideration of all of these factors by liturgical scholars contributed to a very clear desire for change—to bring the faithful into the enactment of worship. The effects of this desire were felt in efforts to encourage "active participation" and in ways which sought to provide edification, comfort, and strength through shared experience in the rites of the church. The next chapter of the present volume will end with a discussion of the papal *motu proprio*[5] of Pius X, *Tra le sollecitudini* (1903), a document of guidance issued by the Vatican that recognizes the growth and diversity in sacred music at the beginning of the twentieth century, but one whose implications also lie beyond the purview of musicians. Pius's text is also the origin of the phrase "active participation" as it relates to liturgy, a phrase taken up enthusiastically by

[4] An ordinary Catholic Mass according to the rite used between the Council of Trent and the 1960s.

[5] A document issued by the Pope's own volition.

the Constitution on the Sacred Liturgy promulgated by the Second Vatican Council and one which will have a significant effect on this chapter of history, because it helped to form a new consensus on the function of the liturgy across all the Christian churches.

What was this phrase, "active participation," taken to mean? Many twentieth-century liturgical architects were of the opinion that it meant that everyone should regularly have a part to speak or sing, either to make them feel included, or to inspire them to believe what they say, or to empower the voice of the individual Christian. This inclination toward "participation" is reflected in many of the new developments in worship.

WHY WORSHIP?

One important consequence of secular twentieth-century society was that for the faithful, time spent worshipping in church was the main opportunity for shared spiritual activity as well as an opportunity for the entire Christian community to gather in one place in which to share their lives and experiences in a world where, increasingly, other forms of gathering were not guaranteed to do this. In churches where the sacraments (and especially the Eucharist) were highly valued, the mid-twentieth century saw these rites being more explicitly framed as acts of community through which the grace of the sacraments was bestowed on the faithful, who could respond independently and actively by having a role in the celebration. The teaching function of the rites, which now more explicitly included the hearing of logical sequences of Scripture arranged in a revised lectionary, and regular affirmations of belief such as the recitation of one of the creeds, affirmation of faith at such events as baptisms and the reinvigorated Easter Vigil, was another central benefit. All of these principles were aided, in the Roman Catholic Church, by the return of almost all public worship to vernacular language.

WHAT HAPPENED?

In all churches, worship became increasingly interactive, with the "full and active participation" of all the faithful, understood as their taking on actions, words, and artistic expressions according to their abilities and talents, considered to be crucial. In order for the rites to be readily understandable by the widest range of people, and so that all worshippers could make some contribution, they were framed in language and artistic forms with which they could interact and to which they could contribute (in some cases, for the first time); this meant the widespread introduction of the vernacular in place of the Latin liturgy of the Roman Catholic Church, and a diminution of archaic formulations and complicated symbolism for other liturgies already in the vernacular. For Catholics, this was a watershed in two senses of the word: it was a turning-point in the history of lay participation and education about the liturgy, but it was also a point of division, one of the main areas of disagreement among the Church Fathers at the Second Vatican Council.

In the Church of England and Protestant denominations, the effects of the Liturgical Movement had also produced a stronger sense of sacramentality, mainly evidenced by an increase in the celebration of the Eucharist (and in receiving both the consecrated bread and wine by the faithful). In the twentieth century there developed means of expression, following the new theological consensus, which found their voice in orders of service. This sacramental emphasis, and an increased desire for the laity to become spiritually and emotionally engaged with the liturgy, comprised the strongest common ground with earlier periods, especially when the fundamental forms of worship were being so substantially changed.

THE DAILY ROUND OF WORSHIP

Almost every church service one might attend at the present time includes at least some points where there is a dialogue between the clergy and the congregation, often in a call-and-response format in which the minister's part (i.e., "The Lord be with you") is to encourage a response (both verbal and spiritual, such as "And also with you/And with your spirit") from the faithful, in effect putting words of faith in the mouths and hearts of the congregation. This is, to a significant extent, an inheritance of the culture of participation represented by Vatican II, of which it was a part. Such dialogues existed at an earlier time, but rarely were they fully engaged in by congregations. Even within services in the vernacular, no one assumed that a sixteenth-century congregation with no knowledge of the precise texts to be used, no mass-produced prayer books or missalettes in the pews to consult, and little religious education to draw upon, would have known the responses in the first place. The tables in English churches bearing the Lord's Prayer, the Creed, and the Ten Commandments in English bear witness to a desire to put at least those texts in front of the congregation. While services of the Word, such as Morning and Evening Prayer, had retained the essential form (the recitation or singing of psalms, canticles, dialogues, and prayers) in which they emerged during the Middle Ages, in practice these services (where not said exclusively by clerics) had often been dialogues between minister and parish clerk. From an early stage the offices of Morning and Evening Prayer had been the most frequently celebrated in Anglican and Protestant churches, but by the twentieth century there was greater encouragement to prioritize the Eucharist. The largest proportion of text in this service, too, was spoken in monologue by the minister, and even when the congregation received Holy Communion in the form of bread and wine it was not customarily an opportunity for further verbal participation beyond a token amount.

Eucharistic liturgies in the Roman Catholic Church (until 1964) had had a more or less fixed form for nearly four hundred years, beginning with the Tridentine Missal, which had replaced most of the earlier locally-practiced variants of the medieval Mass in the sixteenth century. Concerning the precise form of the service, as with the form of the Eucharist in the Middle Ages, there were dialogues at sung celebrations between the celebrant and others present who sang the Ordinary and the Proper of the Mass, respectively the parts of the Mass which remained from service to service, and those parts which were "proper" to the service of the day.[6] Ordinarily, though, these were chanted by clerics in choir or by lay singers, with the remainder of the congregation engaged almost exclusively in silent prayer or devotion. Attendance at Mass was

[6] That is, texts specifically written to be performed on a particular day.

accompanied by the spiritual benefits of those devotions (forgiveness of sins, blessing, the opportunity to share in a sacrament instituted by Christ) as well as the sacrifice offered by the celebrant on behalf of the congregation and any particular intentions (which dedicated the service to some special subject of care such as a deceased relative). For Catholics, the expression "to hear Mass" had a different meaning before Vatican II—a rather literal one.

Despite the very different theological and liturgical priorities of the Church of England, and the dramatically different form of service, a similar state of affairs had prevailed as to the eucharistic rite: it too had remained largely unchanged since the inception of the Book of Common Prayer, and its form, coupled with long exhortations commanded to be read by the priest, had not been designed to be heard (or interacted with) by congregations with modern priorities and spiritual education. The introduction in 1946 of the Shorter Prayer Book had made some strides in amending the language and the degree of congregational participation. But the emergence of this book, a successful product of an otherwise failed movement for liturgical revision, had not come without a great deal of argument.

PRAYER BOOK REVISION AND THE CHURCH OF ENGLAND

Since its separation from Rome in the sixteenth century the Church of England has always, almost by definition, accommodated a vast array of theological and liturgical preoccupations, ranging from the faith which led John Wesley from Anglicanism to what would become Methodism, to the sacramentality of William Laud, Lancelot Andrewes, and the Oxford Movement. Despite this, before the twentieth century there had been a minimum of substantive change in the actual forms of the Office and of the Eucharist since the introduction in 1549 of the Book of Common Prayer compiled by Thomas Cranmer, the first Anglican Archbishop of Canterbury, a state of affairs perhaps exacerbated by the need to have any changes legislatively approved, owing to the fact that the church remained Established, that is, part of the state with the sovereign at its head. Despite the desires and efforts of the Ritualist camp (those who hoped to introduce more elaborate and sometimes historical forms of worship, especially around the Eucharist), and indeed those who had sought a more prescriptively and inflexibly Protestant expression of belief, the Prayer Book remained the only authorized form of worship in the Church of England. By the dawn of the twentieth century it was felt in many circles that there should be some revision of the Prayer Book, either to settle for a plurality of theological interpretations of the same observance or, conversely, to allow for the elaboration of rites. The Ritualists, in introducing new textual and aesthetic stimuli to the liturgy, some of which particularly appealed to the senses, used a sense of historic faith and piety as one justification: as Walter Frere (writing some time after the inception of the Liturgical Movement) put it, "Many a poor sinner can express his trust in his Divine Saviour far better by kissing his crucifix than by attempting to expound his . . . doctrine of the atonement."[7] Further, on the subject of participation, Frere was at pains to point out that Latin Matins (as practiced in the Middle Ages) provided a "special task" to complete (whether it be reading a lesson or singing the intonation of a psalm) for each of forty or fifty persons, compared with the relatively staid and nonparticipatory dialogue of Prayer Book Mattins and Evensong.

Not all such ceremonial, doctrine, and aesthetic embellishments of the Prayer Book rite would perhaps seem overly Catholic now: among these "popish" traditions, many of which are now typical of Anglican worship, were crosses and candles on the altar (which might be made of stone rather than wood); "Roman" vestments such as chasubles and mitres; the mixture of water and wine in the chalice; reservation of the consecrated elements of the Eucharist; and celebration facing east rather than facing the congregation. Although all of these traditions are now common, none had been known in the Anglican Church until they were "restored" by the Ritualists. None existed by explicit authority in the Prayer Book of 1549, the revision of 1552, or the Restoration book of 1662. The justification for the use of such ornaments as were thought

[7] Frere, *Religious Ceremonial*, 6–8.

"popish" was the so-called "Ornaments Rubric" which appears thus in 1662: "Ornaments . . . shall be retained, and be in use as were in this Church of England in the second year of the reign of King Edward the Sixth," which they interpreted to mean the unaltered ceremonial practices of the unreformed English church. The paucity of rubrics elsewhere left a great deal open to interpretation, since most of the Ritualists' activities were not expressly banned.

In his pamphlet *Protestant Ritualists* (1872), the liturgical scholar and Catholic convert William Maskell described the Prayer Book order for Holy Communion as "a pure jumble, unlike any ancient liturgy which was ever used in the Christian church. The compilers appear to have cut the Sarum ordinary and canon of the mass into pieces, and mixed the fragments with bits taken out of the Middleburg [prayer book] and other forms compiled by protestants abroad, and then taken them, as it were hap-hazard, out of a bag and stitched them together."[8]

On the subject of ceremonial, Maskell wrote that the Ritualists

> are content to be suffered to hold their particular opinions . . . to claim no higher authority than that which sends their next door neighbour into his pulpit to contradict them in every possible way . . . to be allowed to put on copes and chasubles and make "high celebrations" upon the strength of an old rubric which refers to the second year of Edward VI, although they well know that the vast majority of English ministers are no less borne out when they wear unseemly surplices and say the office of communion with every mark of carelessness.[9]

A Ritualist, for Maskell, "admits the lowest evangelical to his communion table because he has no authority to rest upon or to appeal to beyond his own private judgment."[10] Maskell was certainly right at least in the sense that the Thirty-Nine Articles,

[8] William Maskell, *Protestant Ritualists*, 2nd ed. (London: J. Toovey, 1872), 30.

[9] Maskell, *Protestant Ritualists*, 13.

[10] Ibid., 30.

adherence to which all clergy and persons in positions of church responsibility had to affirm, explicitly forbid some of the Ritualist practices. Initial deliberations about the potential reform of the Prayer Book, which took place around the turn of the century, were marked by conflicts between post-Tractarian Anglo-Catholics who wanted vestments and a greater emphasis on the sacraments, and the Protestants who favored a deliberate move toward "low church" and the explicit denial of more Catholic doctrine. It is interesting to note that the fathers of the Oxford Movement in fact preferred the Prayer Book to Roman practices, although this view did not continue to be held by their successors.

Seeking to find a new consensus, in 1904 the British Prime Minister Balfour initiated a Royal Commission which, in 1906, reported that "the law of public worship is too narrow for the religious life of the present generation": in effect supporting an increase in ceremonial and tradition. Until 1927, several committees of the Convocations of the Church of England discussed the areas of potential renewal and change in the Prayer Book, especially where new developments in ritual and liturgy were concerned. The most important misgivings had by the evangelical party were related to the reservation of the Sacrament and, within the eucharistic rite, the introduction of an *epiclesis* (invocation of the Holy Spirit) during the consecration of the bread and wine, as well as moving the prayer of oblation to follow the prayer of consecration (as had been the case in the 1549 rite), both of which were attempts to incorporate historical forms of Eucharistic prayer into the service.

Despite a continued lack of agreement on the part of many bishops, including some who resisted any change at all,[11] the proposed revisions to the Prayer Book were approved by the Church's own governing bodies and passed by legal requirement to the Houses of Parliament, where it became clear that the revised volume failed

[11] Walter Frere compares this type of dispute with the situation in the early church, namely that "[it] was more occupied with carrying out its worship than in discussing, describing, or even formulating it." *The Principles of Religious Ceremonial*, 2nd ed. (London: A.R. Mowbray, 1928), 41.

fully to satisfy either Anglo-Catholic or evangelical interests. Although legislation to introduce the revised form was introduced and passed in the House of Lords, it failed on two occasions, the last in June 1928, to pass in the House of Commons, amid serious criticism that the Established church, including the bishops who had supported it in the Lords, was condoning "popery." The 1662 Prayer Book, which had been issued after the Restoration of the monarchy, remained the principal authorized form of service in the Church of England until the last twenty years of the twentieth century, and remains the only one authorized on a permanent basis, although after the Second World War, Holy Communion increasingly replaced Morning Prayer as the principal Sunday service. As in the case of the Roman Catholic Tridentine Mass, questions began to be asked about the useful engagement of the laity, and the Alternative Service Book (1982) and its successor Common Worship (2000) adopted a eucharistic rite very similar to the new Mass of the postconciliar Catholic Church.

Numerous free churches (those free of institutional oversight, unlike the Church of England) had enjoyed rapid growth and permissive legislation had allowed them to take root in Britain.[12] Similar developments were taking place around the world, and in America, where the "frontier" tradition of worship was strong, camp meetings and other immersive forms of worship, preaching, conversion, and initiation had long been a key part of the Christian experience. These traditions led notably to the "Crusades" of Billy Graham, evangelistic gatherings in large venues such as theatres, stadiums, and arenas, which encouraged people to become Christians, and the growth of charismatic forms of congregational praise associated with many of the denominations developed in twentieth-century America. The very name given to "Pentecostal" worship celebrates the gifts of the Spirit within the people of God, and some of these are made manifest in worship: speaking in tongues, preaching the inspired word, healing by prayer and laying on of hands, and diverse, emotive, and lively music of all sorts. In many of these tradi-

[12] See Roger Scruton, *Our Church: A Personal History of the Church of England* (London: Atlantic Books, 2012).

tions baptism is normally reserved for older children who have reached the age of reason and adults. The regular pattern of worship often includes Communion celebrated from time to time, in a non-sacramental framework of understanding. The congregation is expressly encouraged to participate in many of the forms of worship exercised by the free churches, especially in the form of call and response, affirming statements made by preachers, and participating in the musical or prayer life of the church.

LITURGICAL RENEWAL IN THE ROMAN CATHOLIC CHURCH

The most significant cause of liturgical change, however, was the Second Vatican Council (Vatican II for short), an ecumenical (that is, universal rather than inter-denominational) gathering of Roman Catholic leaders which was called for by Pope John XXIII in order that the church might consider seriously the future of its interactions with the modern world. The council, convened between 1962 and 1965 in four sessions, sought to engage with the new theological stance that embraced a church moving together with the experiences of a changing social, political, and cultural environment, as well as with the desire to be inspired by the writings and practices of the early church. Unsurprisingly, the liturgy was one of their greatest priorities.

The council's deliberations had been informed considerably by the already mature thought stemming from the Liturgical Movement, including *Mediator Dei*, a *motu proprio* of Pius XII issued in 1947 that celebrated the renewal of the liturgy and sought to provide some guidance on how continuing revitalization should be carried out.[13] Article 7 of *Mediator Dei* points out that "duty obliges Us [the pope] to give serious attention to this 'revival' as it is advocated in some quarters, and to take proper steps to preserve it at the outset

[13] *Mediator Dei: Encyclical of Pope Pius XII on the Sacred Liturgy to the Venerable Brethren, the Patriachs, Primates, Archbishops, Bishops, and Other Ordinaries in Peace and Communion with the Apostolic See*, The Holy See website, http://www.vatican.va/holy_father/pius_xii/encyclicals/documents/hf_p-xii_enc_20111947_mediator-dei_en.html. Accessed November 15, 2013.

from excess or outright perversion." The enormous enthusiasm for restoring accompaniments to worship, such as plainchant, as well as some of the more inventive efforts at renewal, demanded a strong tone:

> We observe with considerable anxiety and some misgiving that elsewhere certain enthusiasts, over-eager in their search for novelty, are straying beyond the path of sound doctrine and prudence. Not seldom, in fact, they interlard their plans and hopes for a revival of the sacred liturgy with principles which compromise this holiest of causes in theory or practice, and sometimes even taint it with errors touching Catholic faith and ascetical doctrine.[14]

Pius upheld the church's obligations of teaching and encouraging the faithful, emphasizing the fact that worship had to be both inward and outward, but that "the chief element of divine worship must be interior."[15] It is consequently "an error . . . and a mistake to think of the sacred liturgy as merely the outward or visible part of divine worship or as an ornamental ceremonial." Worship, therefore, did not function without the conscious and directed action of the mind and heart "in quest of the perfect life," and true sanctity was not satisfactorily attained except through the liturgy and sacraments observed by the church in communion with Christ its divine Head. The effect of the eucharistic sacrifice and of the other sacraments (response to God's love in Christ and transformation by grace) derives

> first of all and principally from the act itself (*ex opere operato*). But if one considers the part which the Immaculate Spouse of Jesus Christ [a name for the church] takes in the action, embellishing the sacrifice and sacraments with prayer and sacred ceremonies, or if one refers to the "sacramentals" and the other rites instituted by the hierarchy of the church, then its effectiveness is due rather to the action of the church (*ex opere operantis Ecclesiae*), inasmuch as she is holy and acts always in closest union with her Head.[16]

[14] *Mediator Dei*, Article 8.
[15] Ibid., Article 24.
[16] Ibid., Article 35.

Pius was careful to point out that within the life of the church, and in the rite itself, together with the devotions of the faithful, nothing was at odds with anything else, and all contributed to the action:

> Article 36. In the spiritual life, consequently, there can be no opposition between the action of God, who pours forth His grace into men's hearts so that the work of the redemption may always abide, and the tireless collaboration of man, who must not render vain the gift of God. No more can the efficacy of the external administration of the sacraments, which comes from the rite itself (*ex opere operato*), be opposed to the meritorious action of their ministers of recipients, which we call the agent's action (*opus operantis*). Similarly, no conflict exists between public prayer and prayers in private, between morality and contemplation, between the ascetical life and devotion to the liturgy. Finally, there is no opposition between the jurisdiction and teaching office of the ecclesiastical hierarchy, and the specifically priestly power exercised in the sacred ministry.

It remained necessary to affirm the place of Latin as the language of the Western church:

> Article 60. The use of the Latin language, customary in a considerable portion of the Church, is a manifest and beautiful sign of unity, as well as an effective antidote for any corruption of doctrinal truth. In spite of this, the use of the mother tongue in connection with several of the rites may be of much advantage to the people. But the Apostolic See alone is empowered to grant this permission. It is forbidden, therefore, to take any action whatever of this nature without having requested and obtained such consent, since the sacred liturgy, as We have said, is entirely subject to the discretion and approval of the Holy See.

Latin, therefore, was unquestioningly retained. This being true, *Mediator Dei* did not shirk from criticizing some of the anachronistic or overtly historical reinterpretations of the liturgy, which certain segments of the church had tried to readopt:

> Article 62 (on anachronism) . . . It is neither wise nor laudable to reduce everything to antiquity by every possible device. Thus, to cite

some instances, one would be straying from the straight path were he to wish the altar restored to its primitive tableform; were he to want black excluded as a color for the liturgical vestments; were he to forbid the use of sacred images and statues in Churches; were he to order the crucifix so designed that the divine Redeemer's body shows no trace of His cruel sufferings; and lastly were he to disdain and reject polyphonic music or singing in parts, even where it conforms to regulations issued by the Holy See.

It was the principal duty of the faithful to consider what was taking place before them, and to align their thoughts and prayers with those of the Mass. It was in this way that their participation in the rite could be most fully realized:

> All the faithful should be aware that to participate in the eucharistic sacrifice is their chief duty and supreme dignity, and that not in an inert and negligent fashion, giving way to distractions and daydreaming, but with such earnestness and concentration that they may be united as closely as possible with the High Priest.

Sometimes the laity were able to take part in the celebration in a substantive way:[17]

> (article 105) They are to be praised who, with the idea of getting the Christian people to take part more easily and more fruitfully in the Mass, strive to make them familiar with the Roman Missal, so that

[17] The laity were also reassured that the Office was not an obligation for them, although it could offer some benefits: "[The recitation of the Office] is the duty only of the clergy and of religious. The laity have no obligation in this matter. Still, it is greatly to be desired that they participate in reciting or chanting vespers sung in their own parish on feast days. We earnestly exhort you, Venerable Brethren, to see that this pious practice is kept up, and that wherever it has ceased you restore it if possible. This, without doubt, will produce salutary results when vespers are conducted in a worthy and fitting manner and with such helps as foster the piety of the faithful. [article 174] It is Our wish also that the faithful, as well, should take part in these practices. The chief of these are: meditation on spiritual things, diligent examination of conscience, enclosed retreats, visits to the blessed sacrament, and those special prayers in honor of the Blessed Virgin Mary among which the rosary, as all know, has pride of place."

> the faithful, united with the priest, may pray together in the very words and sentiments of the Church. They also are to be commended who strive to make the liturgy even in an external way a sacred act in which all who are present may share. This can be done in more than one way, when, for instance, the whole congregation, in accordance with the rules of the liturgy, either answer the priest in an orderly and fitting manner, or sing hymns suitable to the different parts of the Mass, or do both, or finally in high Masses when they answer the prayers of the minister of Jesus Christ and also sing the liturgical chant.

One of the implications of Pius's new doctrines in the spirit of *Mediator Dei* was the authorization of the introduction of the vernacular in the acts of the church, including sacraments, outside the context of the Mass. In 1948 he established the Pontifical Commission for the Reform of the Liturgy, which oversaw revisions of the liturgical calendar, a re-institution of the Easter Vigil and the substantial modification of the rites of Holy Week. It was with this atmosphere of liturgical experimentation and renewal that, almost immediately upon his election, in January 1959, Pius's successor Pope John XXIII announced his intention to summon an ecumenical council, among the concerns of which was the further revitalization of the liturgical rites of the church.

In advance of the council, new editions of the Breviary and Missal were issued in 1961 and 1962 respectively, with the hope that the current liturgical services would reflect the recent changes, but with the understanding that even more fundamental principles were to be discussed at the council. The work of a Preparatory Commission on the Liturgy solicited input from clergy, church administration, and academic authorities, almost all of whom were agreed that the basic edificatory and catechetical function of the liturgy, which had long been missing, should be restored. Respondents to this consultation were widely in favor of the continued introduction of the vernacular, the stripping-back of accretions onto the basic forms of service which had been acquired over the years, the inculturation of the liturgy in the various social and cultural circumstances in which the church found itself, and the active participation of the faithful in the rites which sustained them. One of the largest setbacks to fundamental change was the continued desire in many constituencies for Eucharistic services, at a minimum, to be in Latin.

The liturgy was the first subject to be discussed in the sessions of the council, and the governing document for matters relating to worship which was produced (*Sacrosanctum Concilium*, the Constitution on the Sacred Liturgy) was overwhelmingly approved by the council, with all but four of the over two thousand voters in favor of adopting it.

Sacrosanctum Concilium illustrated the strong will of the church to renew the liturgy so that it remained faithful to principles but benefits the faithful in pastoral and educative ways, and it was in the liturgical reforms that the *aggiornamento* or "bringing up to date" of the Catholic faith initiated by Pope John affected the laity most strongly. Some of its key objectives were to assist the faithful in growing and learning as well as offering the sacrifice of praise, and for the liturgy to reflect and appeal to all of humankind. These intentions were in agreement with some of the other priorities of the council, such as the revival of Scripture as an active and living part of Catholic life and the affirmation, in the fourth chapter of the Dogmatic Constitution on the Church *Lumen Gentium* (one of the other governing documents issued by the council) of the priesthood of the faithful, exercised through the congregation joining and adding to the sacrifice offered by the celebrant of the Mass. The faithful were encouraged to take up this universal priesthood through their participation in worship and sacraments.

The principles in *Sacrosanctum Concilium* follow on from the basic understanding that Christ is always present in the church and especially in its liturgy; not simply in the Eucharist as sacrament, but also in the work and spiritual sacrifice of priests and in the inspired word of God expounded in Scripture. Consequently, "In the liturgy the sanctification of man is manifested by signs perceptible to the sense, and is effected in a way which is proper to each of these signs . . . . From this it follows that every liturgical celebration . . . is a sacred action surpassing all others,"[18] a state-

[18] *Sacrosanctum Concilium*, in Walter Abbott, *The Documents of Vatican II* (London, 1966), 141.

ment which appears to uphold the prioritization of public worship and the Eucharist which had been one of the central preoccupations of the nineteenth-century liturgical revival. It was critical, then, that the laity should be exhorted to attend all services "knowingly, actively, and fruitfully," not neglecting private prayer or devotion, but with minds focused on the act of celebration. For all, "the very nature of the Liturgy" demands "full, conscious, and active participation," for this is "the primary and indispensable source from which the faithful are to derive the true Christian spirit."[19] In addition to attentiveness and verbal participation at appropriate times, it was pointed out that "at the proper times all should observe a reverent silence." This was to be distinguished from passivity and from overeager verbalization, and perhaps to illustrate the fact that active participation need not necessitate constant responses from the congregation. In terms of their own spiritual engagement, and in order to exercise their own priesthood, laity were also reminded that they "should not be [present] as strangers or silent spectators,"[20] but to "learn to offer themselves too," along with the priest. It was active participation that allowed the liturgy to be instructive, since "the visible signs used by the liturgy to signify invisible divine things have been chosen by Christ or the Church." The rites themselves were to have "a noble simplicity . . . short, clear, and unencumbered." As concerned the communion of the congregation, it was suggested that it was best for the faithful to receive the sacrament in elements consecrated at the same Mass rather than bread and wine previously reserved, presumably in order that the rite maintained its functionality and simplicity.

In a concession to those who had been insistent about the retention of Latin during the consultations prior to the council, the historic language of the church was ordered to be preserved in the liturgy itself, but the limits of what was permissible in the vernacular were to be extended considerably, first in the declamation of readings, then in prayers and chants, according to the prescriptions

[19] Abbott, *The Documents of Vatican II*, 144.
[20] Ibid., 154.

of the "competent territorial authority."[21] This echoes the desire and the need to open "the treasures of the Bible" through more systematic reading, as well as a meaningful and relevant homily.[22] There remained a need for a "warm and living love for Scripture."[23] The laity were reminded that it was essential to attend both the Liturgy of the Word—the first half of the service comprising readings, the homily, and prayers—as well as the Liturgy of the Sacrament. This was ordained in an attempt to prevent the congregation arriving in time for the consecration, a practice which had developed from the Middle Ages onward as a result of the laity placing great emphasis on being able to see the moment of consecration and not on other parts of the service, such as readings or prayers which they could not understand explicitly.

Among other significant changes to worship, *Sacrosanctum Concilium* decreed that the ancient practice of concelebrating the Mass (celebrating with more than one priest taking an active role in the consecration) should be returned to active use. There was also a desire for the "prayer of the faithful" to be represented in the Eucharist in a permanent, recognized form. Concerning other sacraments, *Sacrosanctum Concilium* also reinstituted the catechumenate (a regulated course of study) for adults preparing for baptism and confirmation, and insisted that extreme unction (the anointing of the sick) was not to be reserved for those who were dying, but to be shared with those who might be in danger. Other sacraments and sacramentals were also to be reviewed, revised, or expunged.

As part of the program of improvements which would make possible the edification of the faithful, it was stipulated that there should be compulsory education in the principles of the liturgy for seminarians and others charged with the education of Catholics. The pontifical universities and similar institutions were also encouraged to carry out advanced research on liturgical matters. Music was described as "of immeasurable value" to the experience of the liturgy. It was stated that where possible, the laity should

[21] Ibid., 150.
[22] Ibid., 155.
[23] Ibid., 147.

participate actively in it, preferably using plainchant. Similar instruction for professional and amateur church musicians was also desirable: "Composers and singers . . . must also be given a genuine liturgical training."

Satisfying all these desires in practice throughout the worldwide Catholic Church took a very long time, but certain of the principles could be put into practice with little difficulty. The proposed *motu proprio* of Paul VI under the title *Primitiae* gave specifics of the norms to be "put into effect immediately," and confirmed that the additions or changes to authoritative volumes imposed at that time were to be seen as authentic, and that no one on his own merit alone was permitted to make any further modification.[24] The first of the new norms, and the most wide-ranging, was the instruction of the faithful in the "biblical, theological, and pastoral principles" relating to the Constitution on the Sacred Liturgy.

In particular, it was stipulated that the chants of the Proper and Ordinary of the Mass were not to be read alone by the celebrant. Similarly the prayer said quietly by the priest after the offertory, known as the "secret," as well as words previously said under the breath during the Eucharistic Prayer and inaudible to the congregation, were to be spoken clearly. Prayer "of the faithful" in the vernacular was to take a form, as yet undetermined, but it was intended that "the celebrant or the deacon express the intention and the people respond." The readings were to be delivered in the vernacular, facing the people, and from the lectern. Confirmation was to take place during Mass, and was to be preceded by the renewal of baptismal promises. As for the Divine Office, it was held that the entire Breviary needed to be overhauled in order to be satisfactory for modern use. It had suffered from centuries of stagnation as well as accretions to its fundamental contents. As the council stated, the Office was valued ("sharing in the greatest honor accorded to Christ's spouse"), but not currently appropriate for recitation other than in religious communities. Where possible,

[24] The draft text of *Primitiae* may be found in the Appendix to Piero Marini, *A Challenging Reform: Realizing the Vision of the Liturgical Renewal, 1963–1975*, ed. Mark R. Francis, et al. (Collegeville, MN: Liturgical Press, 2007).

the Office was to be recited together and its texts to be sung as much as possible. The vernacular was allowed for those "for whom the use of Latin constitutes a grave obstacle."

SOME IMPLICATIONS OF VATICAN II

For the liturgy, the Second Vatican Council could only be described as an entirely fresh start, both in what was involved in carrying it out and in the way it was perceived to operate for Catholic Christians. Because, as the constitution had it, liturgy was the summit of Christian activity and the source of edification as well as the source of holiness. Its modification meant that Catholics were very carefully and seriously reconsidering the functions of worship in the outward-facing activity of the body of Christ, the church, and in the relationship between that body and the minds of the faithful. What the council fashioned was a church whose liturgy placed the capacity for response back in the hands of individual worshippers to affirm their faith, to experience the riches of Scripture and tradition, and an environment in which the worship of congregations became cohesive with the concerns and the cultural backdrop of the ethnic and political communities in which they existed. These effects were not felt in the Catholic Church alone, but were the source and inspiration for continued thoughtful consideration of the role of worship within spiritual life and in the modern world across all Christian denominations where "active participation" might have seemed to be lacking.

The continuing task of revision of the texts incorporated a rewriting and reorganization of the eucharistic liturgy with much inspiration taken from the practice of the early church. When these rites were complete they were translated into a wide range of vernacular languages so that, for the first time, Catholics were worshipping with words in their own customary language. Despite the restrictions placed on the use of the vernacular as described in the constitution, it had become clear that only a complete translation of the rite would be suitable to the imperative for congregational understanding and participation.

The rediscovered centrality of the Bible as the inspired Word, as well as the consequent emphasis on the regular hearing and study of Scripture, encouraged Catholics and other Christians to prepare lectionaries for worship that embraced more of the Bible and made selections from a wider range of books. This allowed for extensive diversity of reading over a three-year period and continuous readings over a number of days from the same prophetic and historical books of the Old Testament. The Constitution on the Sacred Liturgy, in more ways than this, represented an acceptance of some principles associated with the Reformation: the priesthood of all believers had been one concept strenuously resisted by Catholics, as had the need to participate "knowingly, actively, fruitfully." But the adoptions went in both directions: the heretofore perceptibly hesitant stance of the Catholic Church on Scripture which had been a criticism of the Reformers and their descendants had been replaced with a very useful lectionary adopted in part by Protestants as well. The Protestant churches began to consider whether the congregation's role in services was sufficient. Furthermore, the Eucharist began to displace other forms of service in the "liturgical" denominations after Vatican II, and (in the Anglican church, for instance) the Eucharistic vestments, reservation of the Sacrament, as well as the appropriation of some Catholic liturgical forms and rituals such as the Easter Vigil and the Paschal Candle, all encouraged by the Ritualists of an earlier century and long favored by Anglo-Catholics, began to enter the mainstream. Many churches adopted multiple forms of the Eucharistic Prayer, many of which were suitable for particular seasons, circumstances, congregations, and types of worshippers. The very words and structures of the Eucharist, as seen in forms authorized after the 1960s in the Anglican and Lutheran churches, in addition to the understanding (however varied in specific theological interpretation) that the coming together of the community to consecrate and share bread and wine was the central event of the Christian week, both show the debt owed by the worldwide church to Catholic revision.

The Western churches began together to experience modern-language vernacular liturgies in a familiar idiom which brought the Word of God closer to the language of the community. The ecumenical International Consultation on English Texts was founded in 1968 in order to discuss and settle upon forms of the texts commonly used in worship, in addition to the denominational groups which had already been set up to do this, including the International Commission on English in the Liturgy (ICEL), a Catholic group whose work had been adopted by others, including the Lutheran Book of Worship (1978). As women began to be ordained in the Protestant churches from the 1970s onward, amongst other concerns it began to be questioned whether referencing God exclusively in male terms was entirely appropriate.

Yet as the church universal was beginning to work out, in a remarkably unified fashion, how it should engage with the modern world, the modern world began to react against the church. Although it had been a long time since the vast majority of Western families attended Christian services, the 1960s saw the widespread sentiment of disenfranchisement with institutions.

The years before and after Vatican II were witness to a radical shake up of the *status quo* which captured the sacramental emphasis and the aesthetic of the Liturgical Movement of the previous century, and simultaneously looked forward to a world in which Christian worshippers changed from passive observers locked in their own internal devotions to active participants, soaking up the riches of the renewed, accessible liturgical rites which were a focus for community life, a source of exegesis, and a continuing means of grace. The attempted Anglican revision of the Prayer Book showed that liturgy represented a serious means of identifying one's particular stance. Vatican II inspired the church, both Catholics and others, to embrace elements of the modern world. They could not have galvanized the new forms of participation of the church in the world without the efforts at liturgical renewal and the rediscovery of origins which had their origin in the nineteenth century and the beginning of the twentieth. These developments form the substance of the next chapter.

CHAPTER 2

The Liturgical Movement

> *It being, truly, Our greatest desire that the true Christian spirit should flourish in every way and be upheld by all the faithful, it is necessary, above all else, to ensure the sanctity and dignity of the temple, where indeed the faithful gather in order to obtain that same spirit from its first and indispensable source.*
>
> —*Pius X,* Tra le sollecitudini

If one had attended a Mass in the early part of the nineteenth century, in more or less any Catholic church, a rather considerable and surprising chasm would have been seen between the action at the altar and the behavior of the congregation. While congregations of the present day, urged on (at least in principle) by the admonition of Vatican II to be alert and thinking, are very much caught up in the actions and words of the priest, servers, and readers, all of which are understandable and audible, their nineteenth-century predecessors, in large part denied these auditory stimuli, saw the Mass as a hospitable place for the carrying out of private devotional acts. They offered prayers, read devotional books, prayed the rosary, or even spoke or sang in honor of particular saints and devotions popular with the laity, especially those relating to Christ or the Virgin Mary. Since the action was closed to the congregation both because of the language barrier and because none of it was even intended to fall on their ears or eyes, it was necessary to draw their attention at particular moments such as the consecration by the ringing of the Sanctus bell. Rarely were the congregation encouraged to make their own communion by receiving the bread and wine, nor was this provided for. The sacrifice of the Mass was understood to have been made by the priest alone, as was the act of reception of Christ's body and blood (save after making confession or on one's deathbed, usually very much outside the context of corporate Eucharistic worship), and the participation of the faithful was limited to being present at the priest's sacrifice and perhaps being receptive to the grace of the sacrament from afar.

This scenario, experienced inside churches, was challenged by a contemporaneous intellectual movement, identified as Romanticism,[1] which celebrated the agency of the individual as well as imagination, genius, emotions, and irrationality. Because Romantics sought a necessarily remote and outlying authenticity—often lying somewhere beyond not always imaginary clouded mountains and dark forests—a distant, sublime history and glorious origins for humanity and institutions were admired (and sometimes hopefully constructed). It was not long until church thinkers began to seek a Romantic restoration of the ancient and glorious origins of the Christian story, lost through corruption, chaos, and sometimes war. This was realized in a repositioning of the liturgy within its own long and sometimes forgotten history. The inclination was to seek a more instrumental role for public worship in daily and spiritual life. This meant moving away from pious but inward devotions toward a closer relationship between the most important acts of the church and those who witnessed them, thereby encouraging the faithful to contemplate their own offering and personal contribution, to consider the origin and function of rites and their accompaniments, and to suffuse the whole with a sensation of continuity with the ancient past, which was the very origin of Christian faith and the force which kept it going.

The practical occupations, aesthetic choices, and intellectual discourse of this so-called "Liturgical Movement" existed in line with

[1] Oxford English Dictionary, 3rd ed.: "[a movement] marked by an emphasis on feeling, individuality, and passion rather than classical form and order, and typically preferring grandeur, picturesqueness, or naturalness to finish and proportion." http://www.oed.com/view/Entry/167129, accessed 16 January 2014.

some of the first philosophical investigations of the role of religion in a wider context. Among these were the studies of the social function and origins of religion propounded by William James in *The Varieties of Religious Experience* (1902) and Émile Durkheim in *The Elementary Forms of the Religious Life* (1912). One of the essential elements of James's book is that it seeks to survey the emotional, non-rational underpinning of religious belief and activity, "rehabilitating the element of feeling in religion and subordinating its intellectual part."[2] Durkheim developed a complex thesis about the universal function of religion in society through the sociological study of primitive religions, with the aim to reduce the embellishments of doctrine and ritual in order to discover the simple but essential character of religion in social life. While accepting that "nearly all great social institutions are born of religion," it was also his contention that "the idea of society is the soul of religion."[3]

According to the writings of the persons most associated with the Liturgical Movement, worship was not simply the public output of the church or merely its principal function. Pius Parsch, canon of Klosterneuberg, wrote that it "is also the instrument, or organ, through which God gives His grace to men . . . Therefore [it] has a twofold function: to lead men to a worship of God pleasing to Him, and to conduct His grace to men."[4] Lambert Beauduin of Louvain similarly argued, in opposition to the received view, that worship in fact was constituted by the common action of the people of God and not solely performed by the priest. Many of the movement's principles were based in Beauduin's book, *La Piété de l'Église*. The theological basis for corporate, shared participation in the liturgy was based on a growing consensus that the church should not be considered a legal structure so much as a gathering of the faithful, an expression of the Body of Christ.

[2] William James, *The Varieties of Religious Experience*, ed. Matthew Bradley (Oxford, UK: Oxford University Press, 2012), 380.

[3] Émile Durkheim, *The Elementary Forms of the Religious Life*, trans. Carol Cosman (Oxford, UK: Oxford University Press, 2001), 314.

[4] Quoted in Ernest Benjamin Koenker, *The Liturgical Renaissance in the Roman Catholic Church* (St. Louis, MO: Concordia Publishing House, 1966), 2.

WHY WORSHIP?

Public acts of faith, presented in liturgies which bore the historical pedigree of Christian continuity and which were received thoughtfully by the faithful, found a renewed place in the life of the church and its people as causes for emotional and spiritual intimacy with Christ on an individual level. In the Roman Catholic Church and subsequently in the Anglican and Protestant churches, this may be seen as the product of a revitalized sacramental theology. No longer was it sufficient for the congregation merely to be present:[5] each service was an opportunity for much deeper engagement, a means of reasserting the central role of public worship in Christian life, a task undertaken in part as a reaction to the overprioritization of the worldly implications of Christian living and in opposition to the tendency, at least among Roman Catholics, to practice various forms of private devotion in lieu of public worship in the form of the Eucharist.

WHAT HAPPENED?

To stimulate pious sentiments among the laity it was necessary to find structures and aesthetic forms which were conducive to the engagement of lay (and clerical) persons. Predictably, this was found in a revival of historic practices of the church: newly restored rituals to accompany the authorized rites which necessarily remained in their substance; new life for art, architecture, and music within the liturgy and running alongside it; and the reordering of buildings to stimulate and edify. Research into the ancient habits and worship of the church to inform all these new developments was also necessarily carried out, helped along by a general interest in historical sources and artefacts and their preservation and study.

MEDIEVALISM AND THE RESTORATION OF ANCIENT ORIGINS

Aside from some initial study directed at the early church, it is no surprise that those who were looking for historical models on

[5] "[Catholic] leaders admit that not one among a hundred knows what is going on in the Mass." Koenker, *Liturgical Renaissance*, 46.

which the revival of the liturgy was to be based fell upon the Middle Ages as their key. It was the period immediately preceding the division of the church into many disputing parts during the Reformation, long before the criticism of rationality, and probably the point at which lay piety, at least when measured by observant population, was greatest. There was much surviving evidence for the trappings of medieval religion and for its theology, conserved in church buildings whose original design was clear, in manuscripts and documents ripe for study, in the physical artefacts of worship as well as the art which it inspired. "Medievalism," broadly speaking the appreciation of medieval culture, took many forms, but two of the most obvious branches intersected when applied to religion and worship: namely the antiquarian study of texts, documents, and evidence carried along by the philological project which had accompanied a surge in historical and literary work more generally, and the appropriation of medieval models in (especially) modern thought and artistic endeavor.

The Liturgical Movement was more a series of shared interests and concerns than an organized undertaking. Catholic priest and influential writer Romano Guardini summarized its origin as follows:

> The liturgical movement came into being because it was necessary. Under the influence of modern individualism and rationalism, the worship of the Church with its magnificent forms, lofty considerations, and concentration on the totality of revealed realities, had been increasingly relegated to the background. Spiritual life had assumed very largely a subjective and private character.[6]

Although the revival of historical forms was famously stimulated by work at Solesmes and the Benedictine community at Maria Laach in Germany, the interest in establishing and editing historic forms of service had been long held. Both the Tridentine reform of the sixteenth century and the English Book of Common Prayer

[6] Quoted in Lancelot C. Sheppard, *What Is the Liturgical Movement?* (London: Burns and Oates, 1964), 9.

were based on some study of ancient sources and founded on a number of preexisting forms. Considerable clerical involvement in the editing and publication of historical texts more generally, but particularly with respect to those of liturgical importance, was a commonplace, partly because of the considerable presence of clergy in academic circles more generally. According to Nigel Yates, in Britain in the nineteenth century, those in holy orders accounted for twenty per cent of antiquarian researchers in general. This figure represents for Yates part of a search, from the 1820s onward, for the illumination and renewal of the "Christian Society" of the Middle Ages, a time when, in contrast with nineteenth-century exigencies, religion and politics were not at odds.[7] It was also the time of the establishment of other large-scale philological projects, notably those of the abbé Jacques-Paul Migne, editor of the famous series *Patrologia Latina* and *Patrologia Graeca* between 1844 and 1866. These two monumental sets were part of a fabulously large publishing empire which published a book every ten days for thirty years, an occupation that saw Migne compared to medieval monks who preserved the writings of the Church Fathers against barbarians. Howard Bloch writes that Migne aimed to reverse France's own revolution and "the very conceptual foundation of the Revolution—the secular science of the Philosophes" depicted in the compendious *Encyclopédies* of d'Alembert and Diderot.[8] Many of these projects were supported, if not published, by learned bodies such as (in Britain) the Henry Bradshaw Society, founded in 1890 "for the editing of rare liturgical texts." These associations were modeled on the antiquarian and regional historical societies which had been founded in great numbers in the early nineteenth century. But with Giuseppe Mazzotta, we now begin to question the ultimate satisfactoriness of their aim by reflecting "on the tendentious manipulations and ideological biases of those nineteenth-century masters, who were intent on concocting and peddling specific

[7] Nigel Yates, *Anglican Ritualism in Victorian Britain, 1830–1910* (Oxford, UK: Oxford University Press, 2000), 43–44.

[8] See Howard Bloch, *God's Plagiarist: Being an Account of the Fabulous Industry and Irregular Commerce of the Abbé Migne* (Chicago: University of Chicago Press, 1994), 6.

paradigms of textual origins for the vindication of one sort or another of political primacy."[9]

Within the nineteenth century, we will explore two examples of these impulses put into practice, first in the restoration of medievally inspired, post-Revolutionary Benedictine monasticism and liturgy at the French abbey of Solesmes with the attendant implications for the Catholic Church, and second, the movement which sought to infuse the Church of England with a similar spirit of its origins. Finally we will consider a 1903 *motu proprio* of Pius X which dealt ostensibly with Catholic sacred music, but also had much greater and wider-reaching implications for the function of worship in Christian life. This document, *Tra le sollecitudini*, is reproduced in English translation at the end of this chapter.

THE REVIVAL OF MEDIEVAL MONASTICISM, LITURGY, AND CHANT AT SOLESMES

Synonymous with both the Liturgical Movement and the Romantic search for ancient origins was the establishment of the Abbaye-de-St-Pierre at Solesmes (near Sable in France), re-founded in 1837 on the site of an ancient priory by a former parish priest, Prosper Guéranger, author of two texts which served to encourage liturgical renewal, *L'année liturgique and Institutions liturgiques*. Katherine Bergeron, who has studied the foundation of the community in detail, compares the establishment of Solesmes to other post-Revolutionary actions in France which tried to reconstruct through arts and spirituality a society which had lost both, efforts which were encouraged by Chateaubriand, Montalambert, and Victor Hugo.[10]

After the French Revolution, where existing institutions—especially the church—had been severely damaged, a French intellectual tradition emerged, strongly rooted in pan-European Romantic ideals. It sought the preservation and reinstatement of those institutions.

[9] Giuseppe Mazzotta, "The Poet and the Critics," in *Dante Now: Current Trends in Dante Studies*, ed. Thomas J. Cachey (Notre Dame, IN: University of Notre Dame Press, 1995), 67.

[10] Katherine Bergeron, *Decadent Enchantments: the Revival of Gregorian Chant at Solesmes* (Berkeley, CA: University of California Press, 1998), 4.

Political agitators, among them Joseph de Maistre, considered religion among the strongest sources of institutional power.[11] The architect Eugène-Emmanuel Viollet-le-Duc, a key figure in the restoration of Notre-Dame de Paris, observed the need, if human intelligence were to progress, "to recreate the entire human past, almost as one might collect an extensive library as the basis for further labours."[12] Such a library of human activity would have been sorely needed in France after the Revolution, when many long-standing institutions had been entirely lost. After years of dispute and rejection of the past, a general return to the familiar, whether or not as a basis for further development, must have been an assurance of continuity and consensus. The restoration of the liturgy, as an indicator of that consensus[13] and, perhaps, proof of the immutability of ecclesiastical institutions, attracted much attention, not least because it stood for historical precedent and the former preeminence and influence of the church.

For Dom Guéranger, the universal adoption of Roman practice was the best way to reclaim the hidden treasures of France's ancient history: it was, then, something of a patriotic matter as well as one of significance for the restoration of the church. As had been true for Charlemagne, Katherine Bergeron suggests,[14] the existence of authentically descended rites whose authority was derived from the early church was important for the establishment of such an undisputable authority for the present. Guéranger wrote of the standardization of liturgy as a "holy [and] peaceful revolution,"[15] surely notable and provocative wording for the time.

[11] Cf. de Maistre, *Considerations on France,* trans. Richard A. Lebrun (Cambridge, UK: Cambridge University Press, 1994), 42–43.

[12] For a wider survey of his work see M. F. Hearn, ed., *The Architectural Theory of Viollet-le-Duc: Readings and Commentary* (Cambridge, MA: The MIT Press, 1990).

[13] See Philippe Buc, *The Dangers of Ritual: Between Early Medieval Texts and Social Scientific Theory* (Princeton, NJ: Princeton University Press, 2001), 255.

[14] Bergeron, *Decadent Enchantments,* 11.

[15] Prosper Guéranger, preface to *Institutions Liturgiques,* vol. 3 (Le Mans, 1840–51).

Key to this restoration, but absent in nineteenth-century France, were the communities that had once possessed the greatest knowledge of the genre. The monastic tradition had been lost, damaged by successive regimes that had sought a break with the past. Of some one thousand Benedictine monasteries in Europe in 1750, only 3 percent survived to the end of the Napoleonic period.[16] But Guéranger's own revolution bore fruit: inspired by an appreciation for monastic life and its liturgy, he gained permission to establish a religious house in France for the first time in many years on the site of an eleventh-century priory at Solesmes, attaching special emphasis to the performance of the canonical hours as prescribed in the *Rule* of St. Benedict.

While the foundation of the monastery had been important for the restoration of monastic life in a general sense, the monks of Solesmes became particularly concerned with the restoration of a living tradition, complete with plainchant, service books, and the ceremonial of the medieval church, all of which had not previously existed in the lifetimes of the participants. This *renovatio* provoked much attention; in their medieval buildings—supplemented by neo-Gothic additions—the monks of Solesmes quickly became an undoubted voice of authority concerning the medieval liturgy. Their inspiring effect on French society was such that the aging Chateaubriand, who in his *Génie du christianisme* had made impassioned arguments for the church, expressed to Guéranger the wish to join the brothers as an honorary member of the community.[17]

In 1883, a meeting of ecclesiastical authorities and chant scholars at Arezzo, urged on by developments at Solesmes, released a set of resolutions criticizing the "deplorable condition" of the liturgy owing to "the divergent and incorrect choir books being used in the churches" and urging "the greatest encouragement . . . and the widest distribution . . . [for] studies and theoretical works . . . which bring light to bear on the masterworks of the liturgical

[16] David Knowles, *Christian Monasticism* (London: Weidenfeld and Nicolson, 1969), 170.

[17] Bergeron, *Decadent Enchantments*, 13.

tradition."[18] Ideas of such a magisterial tradition must have come naturally. Charlemagne's efforts to produce uniformity in liturgical practice were a historical precedent, as were those of the Council of Trent. The notion of a centralized liturgical authority, too, must have had Tridentine origins. To seek some fundamental, mysterious perfection in the past was a tenet of the Romantic movement. All of these principles saw their application in an ecclesiastical context at Solesmes.[19]

Guéranger and his followers believed that the most useful and authentic realization of the desired flavor of Benedictine spirituality could be achieved through accurate reconstruction not only of the buildings and administrative structure of the community, but also of its worship and music. The function of all these historic forms was to rediscover the aesthetic, emotional, sensory source of the praiseworthy piety of bygone days.

To this end, a growing number of scholar-monks were commissioned to probe the earliest medieval sources, although their efforts were influenced by two different approaches propounded by two of the monks of Solesmes. Dom Joseph Pothier was in favor of an aesthetic approach to the chant itself and a preference for more ancient sources, while his colleague Dom André Mocquereau

[18] Resolutions of the Arezzo Congress, 1883, reproduced in Appendix I of Pierre Combe, *The Restoration of Gregorian Chant: Solesmes and the Vatican Edition*, trans. Theodore N. Marier and William Skinner, (Washington, DC: CUA Press, 2003).

[19] While it may be conventional to regard the development of Solesmes merely as a Romantic occupation, the historiography of its foundation is worth mentioning. In a memorable review of Katherine Bergeron's recent history of Solesmes, Peter Jeffery suggests that she departs from the usual story, for Solesmes is explained in one of two ways in earlier accounts: either as a story of "triumph in adversity," "restoring monasticism to post-Revolutionary France and ultramontane Romanism to a church beset by Jansenist neo-Gallicanism," or one in which Guéranger is described as "a 19th century forerunner of the 20th century liturgical movement," a proponent of renewal and congregational participation. Bergeron, a scholar who grew up after Vatican II and who was, perhaps, inspired more by historical than ideological motives, illustrates the early leaders of Solesmes as men of their time.

preferred a critical, almost philological approach.[20] But the quantitative approach to history had long roots. Since the beginning of the Napoleonic era the French had been preoccupied with surveys and figures, perhaps attributable to a hope that knowing a great deal about society as it stood would help to reform it.[21] The statistician Adolphe Quetelet proposed a *homme moyen*, a model which, later adopted both by Marx and Durkheim, "exhibited all human attributes in a given country." Regardless of the difficulties associated with surveying an entire population, Quetelet believed that an "average" model would aptly illustrate broad societal characteristics.[22] The Annales school may have leaned on this heritage. Not only was it possible to survey the *longue durée* quite easily through comparison of figures (i.e., rents, unemployment) over time, but also to overlook ambiguity in specific cases while using statistical generalizations to construct the broader picture.

In any case, the overall methodology had been anticipated by the community's first abbot: "One possesses the pure Gregorian phrase [if] the versions from many disparate churches agree," Dom Guéranger had written.[23] The establishment of authoritative forms of service in the style of performing editions was a necessary condition for the success of the enterprise. "Solesmes guards an unchangeable idea," claimed Dom Gregorio Suñol (monk of Montserrat), "and in order to apprehend it rightly we must free ourselves from the tyranny of fashion, acquire the Gregorian temperament and recapture the antique soul."[24]

In seeking authoritative, historically informed models for the appropriately authentic performance of Mass and Office in their own community, the monks of Solesmes were ascribing to these forms

[20] Bergeron, *Decadent Enchantments*, 93.

[21] Alain Desrosieres, *The Politics of Large Numbers: A History of Statistical Reasoning* (Cambridge, MA: Harvard University Press), 33.

[22] Described in Pat Hudson, *History By Numbers* (London: Hodder, 2000), 37.

[23] « On possède la phrase grégorienne dans sa pureté [si] les exemplaires de plusieurs églises éloignées s'accordent. » Prosper Guéranger, *Institutions Liturgiques*, 3 vols. (Mans, 1840–51), 1:306.

[24] Gregorio Suñol, *Text Book of Gregorian Chant According to the Solesmes Method*, trans. G.M. Durnford (Tournai: Desclýýe & Co, 1930), vii.

the legitimacy which the refounded monastery sought. Aside from the practicalities of having a form of worship suitable to their way of life, for Solesmes the function of the liturgy in observing the Mass and Hours as its predecessors had done was to appropriate the historical authority of the liturgy to legitimate the existence and practices of a recently established monastery. It was perhaps for this reason that they were carefully redacting texts and melodies so as to derive maximal benefit.

A MEDIEVAL LITURGICAL IDENTITY FOR THE CHURCH OF ENGLAND

Michael Alexander writes that "in no other country [than England] does the Medieval Revival seem as central, perhaps because the origins of the English church, monarchy, and Parliament . . . are medieval."[25] As at Solesmes, the origins of quantitative, evidence-based philological work for medieval texts had long been laid: Stuart Piggott writes that the necessary conditions for the scholarly study of antiquities had been produced by the seventeenth century, as a result of the "nascent scientific disciplines."[26] More importantly, Piggott points to the rise in interest in the later sixteenth century for purposes of national unity and identity, in the Anglo-Saxon period, which he suggests to have been an attempt to underpin "the new fabric of government and society." Alexander also points out that the Elizabethan church was very much in pursuit of evidence that the church *in* England had always had a degree of independence from Rome dating back to the earliest days of Christianity in England.[27] If there was a central motivation behind the multifarious efforts toward the reconstruction of the texts and the music—as well as the architectural and material trappings—of the medieval church in Britain, it was in many cases the same: namely, the editors were seeking to provide the proof of a distinct and

[25] Michael Alexander, *Medievalism: The Middle Ages in Modern England* (New Haven, CT: Yale University Press, 2007), xxi.

[26] Stuart Piggott, *Ruins in a Landscape: Essays in Antiquarianism* (New York: Columbia University Press, 1976), 20.

[27] Alexander, *Medievalism*, 59, 64.

self-sufficient insular component of the universal church. If a sufficiently ancient distinctive liturgical dialect could be identified, the English church's claims to a greater independence would be strengthened.

This search for a renewed and unified Christian origin, following the Catholic Relief Act 1829 (the final repeal of all anti-Catholic legislation in Britain), represented a striving for a past time when religion was not controversial or divisive, an important task for the Victorian scholar-priest. In practice, the fruits of antiquarian labors were also part of the evidentiary basis for interpretations, modifications, and augmentations of the Prayer Book liturgy. Justification for these changes through historical precedent could be found, according to the ritualists, in the "Ornaments Rubric" promulgated in the 1559 Elizabethan recension of the Prayer Book:

> the chauncels shall remain, as they have done in tymes past. And here is to be noted, that the Minister at the time of the communion, and at all other tymes in hys ministracion, shall use suche ornamentes in the church, as wer in use by aucthoritie of parliament in the second yere of the reygne of king Edward the VI.[28]

The "catholic" nature of the Elizabethan prayer book has also been linked to its words of administration at Holy Communion,[29] not to mention the fact that it seems to reintroduce an understanding of the sacraments that was suppressed in the first and second Prayer Books of Edward VI, volumes which betray a more ardently Protestant theology, suppressing the idea that the Communion service was more than a bare memorial. It is easy to see why the so-called "Ritualists," proponents of a liturgy with ritual embellishments, would have seen the Ornaments Rubric as an authoritative justification for the reintroduction of pre-Reformation decoration, vestments, and architecture, and by extension liturgical accompaniments such as appropriate music and liturgical amendments. The uncovering of a rite with apparently ancient origins,

[28] From the order for Morning Prayer, in the Book of Common Prayer, 1559.

[29] Eamon Duffy, *The Stripping of the Altars: Traditional Religion in England 1400–1580* (New Haven, CT: Yale University Press, 1992), 567.

based on evidence from several surviving examples of the earliest known English liturgy, would be very advantageous as a proof of the catholicity of the church itself. The natural approach to this issue would be an editorial project of the sort that has been described, with its objective being the synthesis of the earliest, most authoritative text, and with the act of its creation taking precedence over the collation of several different versions and attention to their diversity. With a view to apostolicity, an ancient and preferably Roman origin for the English liturgy would be highly desirable.

Among the various Anglo-Catholic parties, Ritualists were for the elaboration of ritual similar to that of the Roman Catholic Church, although the particular expression of this desire fell into two camps: those who were in favor of adopting *contemporary* Roman Catholic aesthetics and practice, and those who, like the Reverend Percy Dearmer, vicar of St. Mary's Primrose Hill and author of the *Parson's Handbook*,[30] propounded a distinctively English realization of the liturgy and arts of the pre-Reformation church. Not all, of course, were Ritualists, or Ritualists alone. High-churchmen had a particular concern for the apostolic succession and authority of bishops and priests, and for the grace conveyed by the sacraments, which were celebrated in the context of formal worship. Tractarians, by definition, were those who were in particular sympathy with the membership and views of the Oxford Movement and its *Tracts for the Times*, which sought to rediscover the apostolic heritage of the Church of England. All of these parties looked, with their own particular motivations, to the establishment of continuity of the Church of England from the medieval church, and so the conditions were set for very considerable scholarly attention directed to the subject and, in fact, no small reliance on the establishment of the particular characteristics of pre-Reformation worship in England.

No matter the title ascribed to them, these efforts to reconstruct the trappings of the medieval English church were not solely an

[30] Percy Dearmer, *The Parson's Handbook: Containing Practical Directions Both for Parsons and Others as to the Management of the Parish Church and Its Services According to the Anglican Use, as Set Forth in the Book of Common Prayer*, 12th ed. (London, 1932).

aesthetic adjunct to a wider theological program. In fact, they were seen as vital, since their historical subject and exemplar had engaged the unlettered, uncultured, medieval layman with ceremonial, music, and art found in its liturgies, buildings, and other trappings of worship. This stance was embraced in particular by the Cambridge Camden Society, later the Ecclesiological Society.[31] Aside from the widely held aspiration for the medieval, and therefore compelling, trappings of church, the Camden Society held the belief that a church which claimed a long and unbroken history stretching back to the Middle Ages should have appropriate church buildings and fixtures. Founding members John Mason Neale (better known for his contributions to hymnody) and Benjamin Webb, despite their relative youth, were (to Stuart Piggott) "vehement, tactless, and arrogant," with a "hideous consciousness of their own liturgical superiority."[32] The Ecclesiologists employed quantitative (read: positivist) methods to derive their desired model: "The only safe way to arrive at any general principles," they wrote, "is to observe and describe the details . . . and from a large collection of such observations, if carefully recorded, much advantage may accrue to the science."[33]

Following on from the architectural and textual "archaeology" and reconstructive labor, a rediscovery of the plainchant that was an essential component of normative medieval worship was also warranted. Chant was to be a tangible expression of theological emphases; it was, "to some extent, the aesthetic realization of high churchmanship."[34] The revival in the Anglican Church was also concomitant with the reestablishment of plainchant in Roman Catholic churches in Britain after the gradual repeal over the eighteenth century of the laws that prevented public Catholic worship. In some respects, and particularly in some corners where the

[31] There is a substantial account of the Society and its activities in James F. White, *The Cambridge Movement: The Ecclesiologists and the Gothic Revival* (Cambridge, UK: Cambridge University Press, 1962).

[32] Piggott, *Ruins in a Landscape*, 178.

[33] White, *The Cambridge Movement*, 50.

[34] Bennett Zon, *The English Plainchant Revival* (Oxford, UK: Oxford University Press, 1999), 251.

restoration of medieval church practices necessitated a Protestant justification, the church was also reestablishing the practice of Archbishop Cranmer, who had ordered "the ancient Plain-Song"[35] to be added to the First Prayer Book of Edward VI (1549). Not all were in sympathy with this restoration, however. Of one parochial visit, the high-churchman and future archbishop Edward White Benson wrote, "All the music was Gregorian, gloomy."[36] This stance, underlining an assessment of plainsong as otherworldly (and hence abstruse), through the dissimilarity of plainsong to contemporary forms of sacred and secular music, was completely contradicted by opinions such as those of the Catholic convert (and Oxford contemporary of John Henry Newman) the Rev. Henry Formby, who in 1848 suggested that it was this very character that made chant suitable to its purpose—namely, an exposition of the mystery of faith.[37]

The enormous interest in Sarum Use may be attributed, at least in part, to the fact that it was an identifiable and historically viable, as well as irrefutably English, dialect of the liturgy of the medieval church, and a vital part of the heritage of the (catholic) Church of England. Dom Anselm Hughes, a long-term member of the Council of the Plainsong and Medieval Music Society, wrote that the society "usually worked on the principle that there is quite enough with which to occupy ourselves in our own territory."[38] Indeed, a tremendous amount of time and money was devoted to the production of Walter Howard Frere's *Antiphonale Sarisburiense* and the corresponding *Graduale*, both of which were issued in fascicles over a substantial period, under the direction of the "small but

[35] Thomas Helmore, *Plain-Song* (London, 1877), 53.

[36] Yates, *Anglican Ritualism*, 179.

[37] Zon, *The English Plainchant Revival*, 235. One advertisement for recordings of chant read: "[Gramophone records] will be the allies of choirmasters, teaching choirs to interpret with exactitude the melodies which the *Motu Proprio* prescribes. By the aid of science, the literal voice of the Church may be heard in the land." Printed in Katherine Bergeron, *Decadent Enchantments*, 134.

[38] Anselm Hughes, *Septuagesima: Reminiscences of the Plainsong and Mediaeval Music Society, and of Other Things, Personal and Musical* (London, Plainsong & Mediaeval Music Society, 1959), 16.

learned group of 'Sarum' scholars who formed [the] inner council,"[39] a state which meant the Society by 1926 was "little more than a propaganda group for adopting the Sarum chant (and no other) for English words."[40] (Hughes does point out that enthusiasm was dampened somewhat by the discovery that Sarum was very much Norman in origin.[41]) Similar sentiments are found in the words of Thomas Helmore, leading light in the Gregorian Association and master of the Children of the Chapel Royal, who argued that "the people's chant" should be "the same kind vocally now as in any century before us."[42] He argued that the "usages and traditions handed down from age to age" should not have been avoided simply because of the English Reformation.[43] "In our opinion," confirmed the *Ecclesiologist*, journal of the Ecclesiological Society, "the Plain Song of the Church is not only the most right, and the most beautiful method, of praising God, but also practically the most easy."[44]

The proposed restoration of historically informed ritual, ceremonial, and music to the modern Church of England was not only a means of inspiring devotion on the order of that experienced in the late Middle Ages, it was also a source of distinct identity and independent authority for a church which claimed apostolicity, but had avowedly broken away from the Catholic Church which claimed the same. The sometimes emotional or spiritual connection between subject and researcher, as present for modern scholars as for the monks of Solesmes, is identified again by Katherine Bergeron, who felt a particular affinity for her topic: "I felt I was . . . rediscovering my own [tradition]."[45] In effect, while liturgical texts might be

[39] Hughes, *Septuagesima*, 21.

[40] Ibid., 34.

[41] Ibid., 33.

[42] Helmore, *Plain-Song*, 152.

[43] Ibid., 48.

[44] White, *The Cambridge Movement*, 216.

[45] Bergeron writes, "It was a tradition that had slipped by a whole generation of Catholics who, like me, had come of age after the Second Vatican Council, a generation raised on the flat vernacular of the suburban church, with its plain-clothed celebrants and folksy guitar masses. For us, knowledge of the

very fitting and conventional subjects for philological study, the driving force for many who have carried out the work has often been related to a doctrinal or aesthetic objective. For some, the establishment of a fixed and identifiable text of the liturgy of medieval England was an indicator of continuity with the rest of the church catholic (and, in the case of some in the Church of England, the identification of Sarum Use as a particularly insular form of the Roman Rite); for others, the musical and architectural supports to worship were meant to inspire an almost medieval fervency of devotion. These motivations were joined by a pan-Western Romantic rediscovery of ancient, long-lost origins and mythologies. All of these influences produced a scholarly milieu in which the establishment of authoritative editions was paramount. Even if their discoveries were not helping to shape a renewal of liturgical forms in practice, the editions themselves stood as a tangible record of medieval activity, which could be mobilized in order to support a variety of political or doctrinal stances.

THE ORIGIN OF "ACTIVE PARTICIPATION"

The phrase "active participation," as much as it is associated with Vatican II's Constitution on the Sacred Liturgy, in fact has its origin in a 1903 *motu proprio* of Pius X. In response to a growing desire for direction in light of the mixed messages on the subject issued by his predecessor Leo XIII, and under pressure from his musical adviser Angelo de Santi, who sympathized with the monks of Solesmes,[46] Pius decisively responded to the plainchant revival in a very positive way, criticizing the poor quality of contemporary sacred music as "one of the most common and most difficult [problems] to eradicate . . . even when everything else is worthy of the highest praise."

The use of chant was a solution to the musical problem; indeed, the best qualities of sacred music, namely the clarity, beauty, and universality which were to be elements of all liturgy, were "met

---

Latin liturgy had become esoteric, relegated to university curricula" *Decadent Enchantments*, xi.

[46] Bergeron, *Decadent Enchantments*, 130.

most fully in Gregorian chant, which is as a consequence the proper music of the Roman Church, [handed down from the Fathers], which very recent studies have so felicitously reconstituted in its integrity and purity." A sounder affirmation of the value of the work at Solesmes and elsewhere could not be desired. It is interesting to note that under the heading *Types of Sacred Music*, he states that "the more sacred and liturgical a composition for the church is, the more its pattern, inspiration, and feel approach Gregorian melody," and that the faithful should be encouraged to join in, "as used to happen in the past."

While it is addressed primarily to the perceived problems in sacred music, a careful reading of the *motu proprio* will reveal some other concerns together with solutions recommended by the Pope, as well as more broadly liturgical insights. It is necessary, he wrote, to "ensure the sanctity and dignity of the temple" where the faithful obtain the Christian spirit "from its first and indispensable source, through active participation in the most holy mysteries and in the public and solemn prayer of the Church." Pius insists in the second paragraph that nothing at all should "even merely diminish the piety and devotion of the faithful" by way of a distraction or disturbance from the true purpose of worship, implying a connection between the devotions of the congregation who are hearing the service and the contribution to their worship from the sanctuary. He equates the best qualities of sacred music with the functions of the liturgy, namely the glory of God and the "sanctification and edification of the faithful." He bewails the influence of secular and "theatrical" forms of music, and emphasizes the fact that the music must be the servant of the text and of the liturgical ceremony, a point assuredly not lost on those familiar with elaborate classical settings of the Mass where the Sanctus and Benedictus take an extended form with solo singing and long instrumental interludes. Lastly (and in common with his successors), Pius makes the strong recommendation that clergy and all who are responsible for composing and performing liturgical music should be properly educated in liturgical matters.

Tra le sollecitudini had three objectives. It was a reproof to liturgically insensitive musical choices which had proliferated in the several centuries since Trent, which were now thought to be inhospitable to the solemn and informed climate of the liturgy. It was an attempt to encourage and to help influence the result of research and investigation into the early sources of the liturgy in order to inform present practice and recover authentic, ancient accompaniments to worship. Finally, it was an order to local authorities to encourage music-making and to train clergy, musicians, and choirs in appropriate skills and techniques. In this document, music represents the wider renewal of liturgical forms, demonstrates the value of one kind of "full and active participation," and points forward to future developments toward the refocusing of the liturgy on corporate celebration.

The remaining part of this chapter presents a new translation of *Tra le sollecitudini* from the original Italian text, which will help to illustrate its fundamental and wide-ranging implications for worship.[47]

Motu Proprio
Pius X, The Supreme Pontiff
On Sacred Music

Amongst the concerns of the pastoral office, not only of this most Holy See, which through the inscrutable disposition of Providence, We occupy, though unworthy, but of every single Church, doubtless of central importance is the need to maintain and promote the dignity of the House of God, where the august mysteries of religion are celebrated and where the Christian people gather to receive the grace of the Sacraments, be present at the Holy Sacrifice of the altar, adore the most august Sacrament of the Body of Our Lord, and join in the common prayer of the Church in the public and solemn liturgical offices.

[47] I thank Jennifer Rushworth of St John's College Oxford for preparing this translation.

Nothing therefore must take place in the temple which might disturb or even merely diminish the piety and devotion of the faithful, nothing which might reasonably give rise to disgust or scandal, and nothing, above all, which might directly offend the dignity and the sanctity of the sacred functions and thus be unworthy of the House of Prayer and the majesty of God.

We will not deal individually with the abuses that can occur in this regard. Today Our attention must turn to an abuse which is one of the most common and most difficult to eradicate, and which is sometimes to be deplored even when everything else is worthy of the highest praise: the beauty and sumptuousness of the temple; the splendor and careful ordering of the ceremonies; the attendance of the clergy; and the gravity and piety of the ministers that are celebrating. Such is the abuse involving singing and sacred music. And indeed, whether because of the very nature of this art which is itself changeable and variable, or because of successive alterations in tastes and habits throughout the course of history, or because of the ruinous influence that profane and theatrical art has on sacred art, or because of the pleasure that music directly produces and which is not always easy to contain within the proper limits, or, finally, because of the great number of prejudices that in such a matter from being inconsequential creep into and then fix themselves tenaciously even in eminent and pious persons, there is a continual tendency to deviate from the proper norm established by the purpose according to which art is permitted in the service of worship, and which is expressed very clearly in the ecclesiastical canons, in the Ordinances of general and provincial Councils, and in the prescriptions successively promulgated by the Sacred Roman Congregations and Our Predecessors the Supreme Pontiffs.

With sincere satisfaction in Our heart We are pleased to recognize the great good that has been achieved in this matter in the last few decades in this Our own city of Rome and in many churches in Our country, but more especially in some nations, where distinguished men zealous in the worship of God, with the approval of this Holy See and under the direction of the Bishops, have gathered in flourishing Societies and placed sacred music once more in the highest honor in each of their churches and chapels. This good work, however, is still very far from being shared by all, and if We consult Our personal experience and take into account the many, many complaints which have reached Us from all sides in the short time since it pleased the Lord to raise Our humble Person to the highest apex of the Roman Pontificate, without further delay We believe it to be Our first duty to raise Our voice forthwith in reproof and condemnation of all that which in the functions of worship and the ecclesiastical offices is recognized to deviate from the proper norm as indicated above.

It being, truly, Our greatest desire that the true Christian spirit should flourish in every way and be upheld by all the faithful, it is necessary, above all else, to ensure the sanctity and dignity of the temple, where indeed the faithful gather in order to obtain that same spirit from its first and indispensable source, through active participation in the most holy mysteries and in the public and solemn prayer of the Church. And it is vain to hope that in such an aim the blessing of Heaven might fall on us plentifully, when our homage to the Most High, instead of ascending with an odor of sweetness, places instead in the hand of the Lord scourges, which at another time caused the Divine Redeemer to drive from the temple the unworthy defilers.

Because of this, so that no one might from henceforth plead the excuse of not knowing their duty clearly and so that they might be relieved of any vagueness in the interpretation of things already ordained, We have judged it expedient to point out briefly those principles which govern sacred music in the functions of worship and to gather together in a general outline the principal prescriptions of the Church against the abuses that are most common in this matter.

And thus with due consideration We publish *motu proprio* this present Instruction of Ours, to which, almost as a set of legally binding rules on sacred music, We wish with the entirety of Our Apostolic Authority to be given the force of law, requiring of all with Our present written command the most scrupulous observance.

Instruction on Sacred Music

I. General principles

1. Sacred music, as an integral part of the solemn liturgy, participates in its general aim, which is the glory of God and the sanctification and edification of the faithful. It helps to increase the dignity and splendor of the ecclesiastical ceremonies, and since its principal office is that of dressing with a suitable melody the liturgical text which is being put forward for the understanding of the faithful, thus its own purpose is that of adding greater efficacy to the text itself, so that the faithful in such a way are more easily moved to devotion and better prepared to receive within themselves the fruits of grace, which belong to the celebration of the most holy mysteries.

2. Sacred music must as a consequence possess to the highest degree the qualities which are those of the liturgy, namely sanctity and excellence of form, from which springs spontaneously the other characteristic of liturgy, which is its universality.

   It must be holy, and thus exclude any profanity, not only in itself, but also in the way in which it is offered by the performers.

   It must be true art, it being otherwise impossible that it might have on the heart of the listener that efficacy which the Church intends to obtain by welcoming into its liturgy the art of music. But it must at the same time be universal in the sense that, while accepting that every nation must allow in its service music those particular forms which constitute in a certain way the specific character of their own music, these forms must nonetheless be subordinated in this way to the general characteristics of sacred music, so that no one from another nation should, on hearing them, receive a bad impression.

II. Types of Sacred Music

3. These qualities are met most fully in Gregorian chant, which is as a consequence the proper music of the Roman Church, the only music it has inherited from its ancient fathers, jealously protected throughout the centuries in its liturgical codices,

which it proposes as its own directly to the faithful, which in certain parts of the liturgy is prescribed exclusively, and which very recent studies have so felicitously reconstituted in its integrity and purity.

For these reasons Gregorian chant has always been considered the supreme model of sacred music, so that there is therefore every right to set out the following general law: the more sacred and liturgical a composition for the Church is, the more its pattern, inspiration, and feel approach Gregorian melody, and the more such a composition is seen to deviate from this supreme model, the less worthy it is of the temple.

The ancient traditional Gregorian chant will thus have to be widely reinstated in the functions of worship, it being held by all as certain that an ecclesiastical function loses nothing of its solemnity, when it is accompanied by no other music than this alone.

In particular it must be ensured that Gregorian chant is reestablished for use by the people, so that the faithful may once again take a more active part in the ecclesiastical offices, as used to happen in the past.

4. The aforesaid properties are also possessed to a great extent by traditional polyphony, especially that of the Roman School, which in the sixteenth century reached the height of perfection through the work of [Giovanni] Pierluigi da Palestrina and continued thereafter to produce compositions of excellent quality liturgically and musically speaking. Traditional polyphony comes very close to the supreme model of all sacred music which is Gregorian chant, and for this reason it deserved to be welcomed alongside Gregorian chant into the more solemn functions of the Church, such as those of the Pontifical Chapel. Traditional polyphony will thus also need to be widely reinstituted in ecclesiastical functions, especially in the most eminent basilicas, cathedral churches, and churches of seminaries and other ecclesiastical institutions, where the necessary means are not usually lacking.

5. The Church has always recognized and favored the progress of the arts, accepting in the service of worship all that which

genius has managed to uncover that is good and beautiful throughout the centuries, bearing liturgical laws always in mind however. As a consequence more modern music is in fact allowed in church, since it too offers compositions of such distinction, seriousness, and gravity, that they are far from unworthy of the liturgical functions.

Nonetheless, since modern music is written chiefly for profane use, the greatest care will have to be taken to ensure that musical compositions in a modern style which are allowed in church do not contain anything profane, do not recall motifs adopted in theatres, and are not shaped even in their external forms according to the pattern of profane pieces.

6. Amongst the various types of modern music, the theatrical style, which was the height of fashion in the last century, especially in Italy, seems to be less suitable as an accompaniment to the functions of worship. By its very nature it presents the greatest opposition to Gregorian chant and traditional polyphony and thus also to the most important law of all good sacred music.[48] Moreover, the intrinsic structure, rhythm, and the so-called conventionalism of this style do not lend themselves, save for poorly, to the demands of true liturgical music.

III. Liturgical Text

7. The proper language of the Roman Church is Latin. It is thus forbidden in the solemn liturgical functions to sing anything whatsoever in the vernacular; and even more forbidden then to sing in the vernacular the variable or common parts of the Mass or Office.

8. The texts that can be set to music being for every liturgical function fixed, as well as the order in which they must appear, it is not permissible either to confuse this order, or to substitute for the texts prescribed any others of personal choice, or to omit these texts either entirely or even only in part, unless the liturgical rubrics allow the organ to supply a few verses of the

[48] The translation published in the *Tablet*, 2nd January 1904, pp. 9–11, omits the word "sacred" from this phrase.

text, these verses simply being recited in the choir. It is only permitted, as is the proper habit of the Roman Church, to sing a motet to the Blessed Sacrament after the Benedictus at solemn Mass. It is however permissible, after the prescribed Offertory of the Mass has been sung, to perform, in the time that remains, a short motet with words approved by the Church.

9. The liturgical text must be sung as it is written in the books, without changing or delaying any words, without undue repetition, without splitting syllables, and always so as to be intelligible to the faithful who are listening.

IV. External Form of Sacred Compositions

10. The individual parts of the Mass and Office must maintain even musically the concept and form that ecclesiastical tradition has given to them, and which was found to be very well expressed in Gregorian chant. An introit, gradual, antiphon, psalm, hymn, *Gloria in excelsis*, etc., must all thus be composed differently.

11. In particular the following rules are to be noted:

   a. The Kyrie, Gloria, Credo, etc. of the Mass must maintain the unity of composition which is proper to their text. It is thus not permissible to compose them as separate pieces, so that each of these pieces might form a complete musical composition by itself and thus might be detached from the remainder and be substituted with another piece.

   b. In the Office of Vespers the instructions of the *Caerimoniale Episcoporum* must normally be followed, which prescribe Gregorian chant for psalmody, and allow figured music for the verses of the Gloria Patri and for the hymn.

   It will, nonetheless, be permissible, on major solemnities, to alternate the Gregorian chant of the choir with so-called fauxbourdons or with verses conveniently composed in a similar way.

   Single psalms are also sometimes allowed to be entirely set to music, providing that in such compositions the proper form of psalmody is preserved; that is, providing that the singers seem to sing psalms amongst themselves, either with new motifs, or with those taken from Gregorian chant, or according to motifs which imitate Gregorian chant.

So-called psalms "di concerto" remain thus forever excluded and prohibited.

c. In Church hymns the traditional form of the hymn is to be preserved. It is thus not permissible for instance to compose a *Tantum ergo* so that the first stanza would resemble a romance, a cavatina, an adagio, and the *Genitori* an allegro.

d. The antiphons of Vespers must ordinarily be set according to their own Gregorian melody. If however in a special case they were to be set to music, they must never have the form of a concert melody, nor the fullness of a motet or a cantata.

V. Singers

12. Apart from the melodies which belong to the celebrant at the altar and to the ministers, the which melodies must always be sung only in Gregorian chant without any organ accompaniment, all the rest of the liturgical singing belongs to the choir of Levites, and thus singers in church, even if they are laymen, act truly as the ecclesiastical choir. As a consequence the music which is chosen must, at least mainly, preserve the character of choral music.

    This does not mean that solos are absolutely excluded. But the solo voice must never dominate in the function, so that most of liturgical text be performed in this manner; rather the solo voice must act as a simple melodic signal or cue and must be closely linked to the rest of the choral composition.

13. From this same principle it follows that singers in church have a true liturgical office and thus women, being incapable of assuming such an office cannot be admitted to be part of the choir or the musical chapel. If thus it is desirable to make use of the high voices of sopranos and contraltos, these parts must be sung by boys, according to the ancient use of the Church.

14. Finally the men admitted to be part of the chapel of the church must be of renowned piety and probity of life, so that, with their modest and devout deportment during the liturgical functions, they may show themselves to be worthy of the holy office they are fulfilling. It will be suitable for the singers, while they are singing in church, to wear ecclesiastical dress and cotta, and if they find themselves too much exposed to the eyes of the public in the choir, let them be protected by gratings.

VI. Organ and Musical Instruments

15. Although the proper music of the Church is purely vocal music, nonetheless music with organ accompaniment is also permitted. In some special cases, within appropriate limits and with the proper care, other instruments may also be permitted, but never without the special licence of the Ordinary, in conformity with the prescription of the *Caerimoniale Episcoporum*.

16. Since the singing must always be at the forefront, the organ and instruments must simply support it and never overwhelm it.

17. It is not permissible to have long preludes before the singing, nor to interrupt the singing with "intermezzo" pieces.

18. The playing of the organ in accompaniments to the singing, in preludes, interludes, and the like, must not only be executed according to the proper nature of the instrument, but must participate in all the qualities characteristic of true sacred music and which have been listed above.

19. The use of the piano in church is forbidden, as well as the use of loud or strident instruments, such as drums, bass drums, cymbals, bells, and the like.

20. It is strictly forbidden for so-called musical bands to play in church; and only in some special cases, provided that the Ordinary consents, will it be permitted to admit a limited, judicious selection, suitable to the surroundings, of wind instruments, so long as the composition and the accompaniment to be played are written in a style that is entirely serious, suitable, and similar to that of the organ.

21. In processions outside church a musical band may be permitted by the Ordinary, so long as pieces that are in no way profane be performed. It would be desirable on such occasions for the musical band to limit itself to accompanying some spiritual songs sung in Latin or the vernacular by the singers or the pious congregations that are taking part in the procession.

VII. Length of Liturgical Music

22. It is not permitted, for reasons of singing or playing, to make the priest wait at the altar for longer than the liturgical ceremony requires. According to the ecclesiastical prescriptions, the Sanctus of the Mass must be completed before the elevation, and thus the celebrant must also consider the singers at this point. The Gloria and Credo, as in the Gregorian tradition, must be relatively short.

23. In general it is to be condemned as a most serious abuse that in ecclesiastical functions the liturgy appear secondary to and almost in the service of the music, whereas in truth the music is merely part of the liturgy and its humble handmaiden.

VIII. Principal Means

24. For the precise execution of that which has hereby been established, the Bishops, if they have not already done so, must institute in their dioceses a special commission composed of people who are truly competent in sacred music to whom, as they shall judge it most opportune, the task of supervising the music which is performed in their churches will be entrusted. Nor should they take care only that the musical works be good in themselves, but also that they match the forces of the singers and that they are always performed well.

25. In the seminaries of clerics and in ecclesiastical institutions, according to the Tridentine prescriptions, everyone must cultivate diligently and affectionately the previously commended traditional Gregorian chant, and the superiors must in this matter generously encourage and praise the young people for whom they are responsible. Similarly, where it is possible, the

foundation of a Schola Cantorum amongst clerics should be promoted for the performance of sacred polyphony and good liturgical music.

26. In the usual lessons of liturgy, morals, and canon law that are given to theology students, those points that more particularly concern the principles and rules of sacred music should not fail to be covered, and the doctrine should be rounded off with specific teaching about the aesthetics of sacred art, so that clerics do not leave the seminary lacking in all these ideas, which are so necessary for attaining a thorough education in ecclesiastical culture.

27. Let care be taken to reestablish, at least in principal churches, the ancient Scholae Cantorum, as has already been carried out most fruitfully in a good number of places. It is not difficult for zealous clergy to establish such Scholae even in smaller and rural churches, in fact they would find in these an easy way of gathering around themselves boys and men, to their own advantage and for the edification of the people.

28. Let higher schools of sacred music where they already exist be supported and promoted as much as possible, and let such schools be founded where they are not yet in existence. It is of the utmost importance that the Church itself see to the teaching of its choirmasters, organists, and singers, according to the true principles of sacred art.

IX. Conclusion

29. Lastly, choirmasters, singers, people of the clergy, superiors of seminaries, ecclesiastical institutions, and religious communities, parish priests and rectors of churches, canons of collegiate churches and cathedrals, and above all diocesan ordinaries are advised to favor with all their zeal these judicious reforms, which have been long desired and are called for by all with one voice, so that the authority of the Church, who has repeatedly proposed these reforms and who now once more inculcates them, be not held in contempt.

CHAPTER 3

Reformations and the Council of Trent

O Thou who camest from above,
The pure celestial fire to impart,
Kindle a flame of sacred love
On the mean altar of my heart.
—Charles Wesley

The Introduction to this volume began with the aphorism *lex orandi, lex credendi* (the law of prayer is the law of belief), attributed to the fifth-century patristic writer Prosper of Aquitaine. While this principle is without doubt true for the entire history of Christian worship, it rings true particularly for the period of reform in the sixteenth century (variously described as "the" Reformation—that is, the Protestant Reformation—and the "Counter-" or Catholic Reformation). This was, it is worth remembering, the first time at which the West possessed more than a single (universal, Catholic) church, and the first point at which related branches of the Western church, once united under the Catholic banner, needed to discover new identities, both doctrinal and public. Changes in liturgy, which more obviously than many other changes laid down the boundaries between the dividing wings of the church, necessarily followed and helped to define the onward course of theological and doctrinal change. The popular understanding of a liturgical rite, for instance baptism or the Eucharist, was always based on the form that it took. Consequently, if the doctrine establishing a rite was subject to change, then its form was also required to change. Throughout all the changes, both Protestant and Catholic, forms of worship were either upheld or modified in deliberately chosen ways, and always reflected the intellectual developments which underpinned the way the rite was to be understood. In so doing, the worship of the various branches of the church helped to forge the identity of the new communities of believers, and the fundamentals of doctrine which needed to be taught to and affirmed by the faithful. The new theological emphases of the Protestants, founded on personal belief and salvation through conscious faith, could be seen in their understanding of the commemoration of the Last Supper, which developed into a "memorial" or "sign" of a sacrifice made once and for all at the time of Christ's death, while the Catholic equivalent continued to be understood as a continuing sacrifice where the body and blood of Christ were actually made present. In all cases those who were shaping worship knew the value of using the most visible, obvious public expressions of their ecclesial life to represent, illustrate, and uphold their theological principles.

WHY WORSHIP?

The glorification of God and the sanctification of the faithful remained the fundamental objectives behind public worship in this period, but for the first time in history, the way these objectives were understood in the Western church began to diverge and the door was open to diverse and opposing official interpretations of worship's role. The functionality of worship depended very much on the branch of the church in question: the Catholic understanding of the Eucharist remained one of sacrifice, with grace bestowed as part of the performance of the sacrament. But a wide variety of alternative interpretations according to the beliefs of the various related but independent Protestant divisions also existed. In both Catholic and Protestant worlds there was a greater emphasis on the use of liturgy as edification, being able to understand the action, and on the removal of distractions from the main purpose of worship.

WHAT HAPPENED?

There was a decisive move away from complexity and legalistic, involuntary practices which did not contribute to the function of a rite. The Protestant churches sought to find simpler forms based on

Scriptural models, with the edification of the faithful made possible through large-scale adoption of vernacular languages. The Catholic liturgy came under centralized control for the first time, and was purged of accretions and complexities which had the effect of streamlining both worship and the calendar according to which it was celebrated, while it remained firmly in Latin. There was a flourishing of liturgical arts, an enthusiasm for reinvigorating Bible-based forms and texts within the daily schedule of liturgy, a reduction of devotional practices, and a refocusing on public celebration. Common themes from previous periods included the continuation of familiar forms of public worship, but with a new emphasis on personal experience and faith.

THE PATTERN OF WORSHIP

Catholic liturgy came under much more stringent controls as a result of its supervision by the Congregation of Sacred Rites in Rome, resulting in widespread practice across the West of the same texts for Mass and Office in all Catholic churches for the first time. There was, by contrast, a proliferation of different forms of service amongst the different Protestant groups, all designed to reflect and uphold the particular agendas of the various churches that had been established. Because these liturgies were consciously different from the antecedent Catholic forms, and sometimes avowedly contrary to them, there was great scope for experimentation and revival. Sometimes these experiments did not coalesce into a fixed form, for instance in the congregations which were built on Lutheran theology. Outside the Catholic Church, the action which took place in the Eucharist began to be understood in numerous ways: as a closed memorial of an event already having taken place; as a manifestation of the Real Presence of Christ without transubstantiation of the physical elements of bread and wine; and in other formulations. These divergent understandings necessarily changed the way worshippers understood the liturgy, and what spiritual effects they believed them to have, which influenced the way they approached the rites themselves.

The following section will explore some of the efforts at reform of the liturgy and the theological disputes which caused these reforms, but it will pay particular attention to the experiences of the

Church of England, partly because that body's experience of divergence from the Catholic Church is very familiar to the English-speaking world, and unique among the movements which had their origin in this period.

Worship and the Protestant Reformers

Perhaps the most prominent figure associated with the pan-European Protestant reform was Martin Luther (d. 1546), a German Catholic religious and theologian who reacted against some of the doctrines of the Catholic Church, especially the absolution of sins by payment, and against the teachings of the earthly church more generally in favor of the view that the Bible itself was the only source of divine knowledge. He believed that salvation could come from faith in Christ alone, which upset the widely held medieval belief that good works had expiatory powers.

In the late 1520s, after his excommunication from the Catholic Church, Luther began to develop forms of worship for the "Lutheran" congregations who followed his teachings. He began with some of the existing medieval orders of service and adapted them to new theological priorities, using familiar texts and hymns where this was possible. It was his aspiration for the services to be celebrated in a tongue familiar to the congregation, but this goal was not immediately realized. The resemblance to the Catholic liturgy could be seen most obviously in Luther's order for Holy Communion. "It is not now nor ever has been our intention to abolish the liturgical service of God completely, but [rather] to purify the one that is now in use from the wretched accretions which corrupt it. . . . So many human inventions were added to [the Mass] that nothing except the names of the mass and communion has come down to us."[1] In practice, Luther favored the retention of the fundamentals of the rite, though cutting down on the number of extra prayers, and with the hope of restoring an edifying cycle of readings in the vernacular. Many other things in the enactment of the service were left to the discretion of the bishop.

[1] Martin Luther, *Formula Missae*, trans. Paul Strodach and Ulrich Leopold, in *Luther's Works* 53 (Philadelphia: Fortress Press, 1965), 20–25.

Of the Office, Luther wrote that daily prayer "serves primarily to train the young and challenge the unlearned," and therefore sufficient interest needed to be introduced into the daily services so that the unenviable situation previously experienced with Latin liturgy, namely nonattendance at the Office through boredom and disengagement, could be avoided.[2] Neither Luther nor the church which bore his name adopted standardized textual forms, however, and unlike in the Church of England, where the Book of Common Prayer became a form of words for the confession of faith, it was more difficult to deduce aspects of Lutheran identity from any widely promulgated rites.

Even fewer fixed forms can be deduced in the case of the Calvinists, whose worship was based around and focused on Scripture. Calvinist worship consciously eschewed any resemblance to the old liturgies. Calvin offered much encouragement to the congregational practice of singing psalms, in contrast to Catholic practice, which he argued was a "murmuring among [the congregation] without any understanding."[3]

Liturgical Change and the Council of Trent

The Catholic Church, which had independently identified some of the challenges to its worship and, with the Protestant Reformation, found its doctrines attacked, convened the ecumenical Council of Trent in a number of sessions between 1545 and 1563. The Council sought to consider carefully many of the aspects of church doctrine and practice which required revision: it issued a considered response to the criticisms of the Protestants and looked critically at areas of faith and doctrine which had been susceptible to abuses. The effects of the council on the uniformity of the liturgy were considerable. In addition to widely promulgated new editions of the Breviary and Missal—which were heavily amended versions of the

[2] Luther, *The German Mass*, trans. Augustus Steimle and Ulrich S. Leopold, in *Luther's Works* 53, 89–90.

[3] John Calvin, *Articles Concerning the Organization of the Church and of Worship at Geneva Proposed by the Ministers of the Council*, trans. J.K.S. Reid, *Library of Christian Classics* 22 (London: SCM Press, 1954), 53–54.

Roman liturgical pattern and intended to reflect the Tridentine deliberations and renewed work to restore the liturgy to a state where it had not been complicated by extensive accretions and local practices—another legacy of the council was the centralization of liturgical authority in Rome in 1588 with the founding of the Congregation of Sacred Rites. This had the effect of placing the Curia, or central church government in Rome, in charge of the form of the liturgy for the first time.

It must be said that the Tridentine reforms had a somewhat less dramatic effect on the liturgy of the Catholic Church than the efforts of the Protestant reformers had exerted on their worship, which had produced new and sometimes surprising forms of service. The Mass remained a modified form of the medieval Roman liturgy, from which had been expunged the creative but distracting efforts of the writers and composers who had extended that form with sequences, extensive resettings of the Ordinary of the Mass, tropes (extensions or altered versions of existing forms), and other ephemeral add-ons. The Office, too, was reordered and consolidated, with more attention given to the lectionary. The removal of votive services for special intentions as well as devotional exercises which had become attached to the recitation of the Office was also mandated. In general, less important observances and saints' days (with which most days in some regional calendars were cluttered) were removed from the liturgical calendar, with the effect that more weekday services observed the continuing cycle of readings and psalms, which followed a logical and edifying sequence. In succeeding centuries the recitation of the Office as well as Mass became an occasion for both clerics and the congregation to assume a largely passive role in favor of the extensive contribution of professional musicians.

Liturgical Change and the Church of England

Given the extremely well-known story of how Henry VIII's "break with Rome" created an independent Church of England with a distinct identity, it may come as a surprise to find that Henry VIII, and the church of which he was head, observed the Latin liturgy to the day he died, and consequently the development of new and distinctive forms of service was not an immediate priority. Rather, it was the Protestantizing of Henry's church after his death which necessitated serious work toward reform of worship and the continuation of policies which had encouraged the gradual introduction of the vernacular into church services. As has been seen, efforts at revision of the liturgy had been made throughout Europe, as reformers, both Protestant and Catholic, saw a need to rationalize the medieval services for Mass and Office. In Henry's own time, revised devotional books, including the "King's Primer," had been printed with royal assent, and in 1538 Thomas Cromwell ordered that Bibles in English were to be put in churches. Contemporaneously, congregations were to be taught the Lord's Prayer, the Creed, and the Ten Commandments in English. Thomas Cranmer, who was Henry's last Archbishop of Canterbury, had begun work on revising the service books of the Latin rite and had produced a first draft, in Latin, of a new version by the time of the king's death. From 1547, liturgical revision accelerated, and a first "booke of the common prayer" was printed in 1549, under the general editorship of Cranmer.

The second part of the so-called Sacrament Act (passed in Parliament December 1547) identified an unsatisfactory state of affairs concerning the reception of the body and blood of Christ in the act of Holy Communion, and condemned the practice of the people receiving only the bread or, as in many cases, not at all. It was, the statute continued:

> more conformable to the commen use and practice bothe of Thapostles and of the primative Churche by the space of Five hundred yeres and more after Christs assention that the saide blessed Sacrament shoulde be ministred to all Christen people under bothe the kyndes of Breade and Wyne, [than] under the forme of breade onelie; And also it is more agreable to the first Institucion of Christe and to thusage of Thapostells and the primative churche that the people being present shoulde receive the same with the preist [than] that the Priest should receive it alone.[4]

[4] "Sacrament Act 1547" The National Archives website, accessed November 11, 2013, http://www.legislation.gov.uk/aep/Edw6/1/1/section/VIII.

The priest, furthermore, was ordered to deliver a "godlie exhortacion" to the congregation to encourage them to receive the bread and wine, and to promise "daunger and indignacion of God" to those who receive it unworthily without examination of conscience.[5] The Order of the Communion, a supplement to the existing form of the Mass, was widely promulgated from March 1548, adding to the typical Latin form of service, as yet unchanged, various texts in English which provided for the reception by the people of the body and blood of Christ. Without changes in the Latin service:

> The time of the Communion, shalbee immediatly after that the priest him selfe hat received the Sacrament, without the variyng of any other Rite or Ceremony in the Masse (until such other order shall be provided) but as heretofore usually the priest hath doen with the Sacrament of the Body, to prepare, blisse and consecrate so muche as will serve the people.[6]

Notwithstanding this admonition that nothing further in the vernacular was to be added, various chronicles report that Mass, as well as Mattins (the Prayer Book's version of Morning Prayer, roughly equivalent to Catholic Lauds) and Evensong (Evening Prayer equating to Vespers), were carried out using additional, unauthorized English-language forms in individual churches before the preparation and publication of the first Book of Common Prayer the following year in 1549. Even the Mass for the commemoration of the death of the King (in 1548) was said in English.

The services of the Prayer Book included responses which could be spoken by the congregation, although these were limited to "Amen" and other matters which did not require either memorization or a written version at hand. Longer texts were said by the priest in the name of all present, and the parish clerk, a lay official

[5] Note that at the same time the house of bishops was discussing the substitution of the vernacular (which might continue the effort to restore the sacrament of Communion to the state it enjoyed in the early church).

[6] Fol. B i verso, in *Order of the Communion 1549*.

who supported the work of the priest, was normally responsible for leading the response to the priest in series of dialogues, as at Morning and Evening Prayer. A rare book in the British Library lays out clearly, with rubrics (instructions), "all that shall apperteigne to the clerkes to saie or syng."[7] Much attention is given to the clarity of the clerk's delivery: the lessons were to be read by the clerk "with a loude voyce, that the people maie heare," while "standyng and turnyng him so as he mai best bee heard of all suche as bee present." Such instructions point to the words of the service not always being well heard in the past.

The first edition of the Book of Common Prayer was intended to supply the Church of England with new, authorized, and precise forms of public worship in the vernacular. While its purpose was to replace the Latin services that had become extensive and increasingly complex in the later Middle Ages, the Prayer Book also became a battleground for the various theological parties in the Elizabethan church, and its contents over several editions reflected the changing doctrinal consensus. Despite the familiarity of some of the texts, Cranmer's work to produce the Prayer Book was no mere translation from the Latin. It condensed services of the Office into two—Mattins and Evensong—and supplied them in a single volume, along with new services for Holy Communion, baptism, confirmation, marriage, the visitation of the sick, and burial, with other "occasional" material and tables of psalms and readings from the Old and New Testaments throughout the year.

The significance of the Prayer Book cannot be overemphasized: it was both a source and a reflection of Anglican doctrine. Here was a document, endorsed by the monarch and by Parliament, which stood as a witness to mainstream Protestantism: it omitted the names of saints, particularly in the Litany which had been until then more or less an exhortation to saints to intercede for those on earth, and it also shared its reforming heritage by its adherence to some form of *lectio continua*, continual reading of sequential excerpts from Scripture. Cranmer's communion service also

[7] London, British Library C.36 d.1, described and with facsimile in John Wickham Legg, ed., *The Clerk's Book of 1549* (London, 1903).

attempted to provide for more frequent reception of the bread and wine by congregations. The suppression of the Prayer Book under the Catholic Queen Mary was evidence enough that it represented to Catholics an insufficient and invalid Protestant invention. Yet its return under Elizabeth stimulated Puritan revolt at its perceived Catholic leanings.

The Elizabethan Prayer Book of 1559 reprinted the text as it was known at the death of Edward VI with some small but important revisions which seemed to the Puritans unacceptably Catholic. Added were the "Ornaments Rubric" which restored previous forms of decoration and ceremonial, and an expanded text to be spoken by the priest at the administration of Communion. Omitted were the reference to the "tyranny of the Bishop of Rome" from the Litany, and the so-called "Black Rubric"[8] at Communion, which had been added to suggest that Christ was not truly present in the Eucharist. In succeeding revisions, some saints were returned to the calendar of feasts.

On the whole, this Prayer Book was received back amicably, although Puritan objections led to public, high-profile criticism. The 1572 "Admonition to Parliament," an anonymous polemic, criticized elements which were felt to be too Catholic, such as kneeling, the sign of the cross, vestments, and ceremonial actions. While these may seem trivial reservations, they were indicative of deeper misgivings, particularly about sacramental theology and reverence to the Sacrament. Later, and despite the best efforts of those behind several efforts by the Puritan camp to expunge all remnants of the Catholic Church from the Church of England, the Jacobean version of the Prayer Book would be seen by many as still more Catholic than its predecessor.

REFORMING AND RESTORING THE LITURGY IN PRACTICE: CRANMER AND QUIGNON

Archbishop Thomas Cranmer (d. 1556) had significant interactions with noted Continental reformers, and his work on the Prayer Book showed the influence of other Protestant orders. In 1536 (the

[8] Printed in black, not in red as rubrics normally were.

year of the execution of Anne Boleyn), Cranmer became involved in the construction of the first statement of faith of the Church of England and its replacement, the so-called "Bishops' Book" or first statement of doctrine, which was presented to the king for consideration in 1538. When Henry rejected its principles, Cranmer opposed his disapproval: the archbishop had by this time embraced the Protestant doctrines of predestination and, importantly, justification by faith alone. But he did not persist in his opposition. Here and at other times, Cranmer seems to have avoided serious royal wrath. He was complicit in the ratification of Henry's subsequent marriages, and was responsible for reporting to him the adultery of Katherine Howard, whom he had forced to confess. The king, in return, showed undoubted loyalty to Cranmer during the "prebendaries' plot," an attempt by conservative clergy to oust the archbishop.

The first fruits of Cranmer's liturgical revision were a vernacular Litany, published in 1544, and the Primer of 1545, both texts that were later to figure in the Prayer Book. It is notable that only after Henry's death were complete liturgical services created in English, and that under the theologically conservative king the forms of Mass and Office would have remained very similar to their Roman antecedents, although references to the papacy and to other matters inconvenient to the Church of England, particularly the feast day of Thomas Becket, were with few exceptions excised from service books by commissioners of the Crown.

It was in the second year of the reign of the young Edward VI that "the Order of the Communion" was promulgated, and deliberations over the contents and form of a wider revision occupied the rest of that year. The Prayer Book in English was issued in March 1549, placating conservatives while demonstrating to Cranmer's fellow evangelicals that revision was taking place. Cranmer's text was said to be inspired principally by the Use of Sarum, constituted by the liturgical patterns prominent at Salisbury Cathedral and widely observed, with varying levels of uniformity, in the province of Canterbury. Other continental forms of service, including an attempt to reform the Catholic Breviary by the Spanish cardinal Francisco de Quinones (known as Quignon), were also undoubtedly influential. The Prayer Book is also notable for the memorable and influential prose style of its author.

During sustained projects of revision and progress, Cranmer continued to face opposition from radicals and conservatives. Failed attempts to initiate a council to debate an international statement of Protestant beliefs resulted in the development of forty-two articles of belief for the Church of England, the basis for the Thirty-Nine Articles which are the foundation of Anglican doctrine. Cranmer also drew up a revision of his original Prayer Book, which distanced itself more thoroughly from Roman practices and doctrines.

Unsurprisingly, Cranmer supported Queen Jane after the death of Edward, and after the ascent of Mary, offered vocal opposition to the reintroduction of Roman practices. Cranmer himself remained free until September 1553, when he was confined to the Tower of London along with bishops Nicholas Ridley and Hugh Latimer, with whom he was later martyred in Oxford.

Some of Cranmer's revisions were representative of more widely observed problems which were also affecting the Catholic Breviary. The notion that the Bible was to be read in a year, spread over the readings for the daily Office, and the Psalms read within a fixed period of time, often a week, had somewhat diminished in the later Middle Ages, and various complaints about these inadequate forms of service had encouraged attempts at revision of the Office. The efforts of Cardinal Quignon in this matter resulted in more than a hundred editions of the revised Roman Breviary before they were superseded by the version arising from the Council of Trent. Years before the development of his Prayer Book, Cranmer, too, had drawn up plans for a revision of the readings and texts of the Breviary (written between 1543 and 1547),[9] attempting to return to the more balanced and Scriptural practices of an earlier time, based in part on the work of Quignon, and elsewhere inspired by Lutheran orders of service from Schleswig-Holstein (1542), Brunswick (1544), and Bugenhagen (1535). Certainly the inclusion of Scripture in English in the Office for the Church of England had

[9] Recorded in London, British Library, MS Royal 7. B. IV, and in John Wickham Legg, ed., *Cranmer's Liturgical Projects* (London, 1915).

authoritative support. The Convocation of Canterbury in 1541 had established that on each Sunday and feast day at Mattins and Evensong the curate of every parish church should read one chapter (in English) of the New Testament to the people, and when the New Testament was finished to proceed through the Old in the same way.[10]

Quignon's revision, itself reacting against the same paucity of continuous Bible readings within the liturgy, was inspired by the situation brought on by the considerable expansion in the Middle Ages of the number of feast days with their own set readings, which meant that even if a rational, comprehensive order for the reading of whole portions of Scripture over time in the Office did exist, it would have been regularly superseded by the texts set for one observance or another, and condensed so as to accommodate the many additional accretions on the liturgical day, namely the observance of votive offices, litanies, and the penitential and gradual psalms. At many of the Hours of the Office, the reading of Scripture other than the Psalms was reduced to no more than a few lines. Often the readings were taken from supposed writings of Church Fathers, not necessarily authentic or identifiable.

Receiving the Sacraments in the Newly Independent Church of England

The Church of England serves here as a case study for the foundation of a church and (consequently) the foundation of its liturgical identity. How did the people, largely ignorant of the machinations and deliberations behind the refoundation of the institution, receive the new public face of the church, a development which they had not necessarily asked for?

For some time after the break with Rome, religious and state authorities had attempted to encourage and impose sanctions of uniformity on the nascent Church of England. In the tumultuous years until the stabilization of the reign under Elizabeth I, numerous injunctions in the name of the Crown and visitations of local bishops attempted to set appropriate standards for parish activity,

[10] Convocation of Canterbury 29 March 1541. See David Wilkins, *Concilia Magnae Britanniae et Hiberniae*, vol. 3 (Gale ECCO, 2010), 863.

especially as concerned material objects commonly associated with popular Catholic or Protestant practices. Whether these pressures on congregational practice provoked the intended effect has been questioned. On one side, supporters of the traditional view hold that the royal injunctions stimulated and supported popular expressions of Protestantism; on the other, it is maintained that the authorities imposed reform on "a population who maintained the traditional catholic religion with enthusiasm."[11] Gregory Dix and Eamon Duffy have suggested that by 1580, many churchgoers would not have known the Roman Rite and would have grown up, privy to "a thousand 'no-popery' sermons," with the new doctrine alone.[12] Yet Dix expressed the belief that "down to 1588, a waning majority of Englishmen passively desired the old rites."[13] Ronald Hutton has gone so far as to say that "the majority of English and Welsh peoples did not want the Reformations of Henry, Edward, and Elizabeth."[14] It is surely difficult to assess the popular sentiment of local communities whose proclivities, unless blatantly in conflict with those of the establishment, must have remained largely unrecorded. To understand how and why these Catholic practices were retained will necessitate an account of what they were, then to explore some of the contemporary documentary evidence.

Among the principal concerns of both church and state authorities were the form and context of the sacrament of Holy Communion. While it had been the summit of liturgical activity in the Middle

[11] Summarized by Fiona Kisby in "Where the King Goeth a Procession: Chapel Ceremonies and Services, the Ritual Year, and Religious Reforms at the Early Tudor Court, 1485–1547" *The Journal of British Studies* 40, no. 1 (January 2001): 65.

[12] Ca. 1570s–80s. See Duffy, *The Stripping of the Altars*, 586–93.

[13] Gregory Dix, *The Shape of the Liturgy*, 3rd ed. (London: Continuum, 2005), 686.

[14] Ronald Hutton, "The local impact of the Tudor Reformations" in Christopher Haigh, ed., *English Reformation Revisited* (Cambridge, UK: Cambridge University Press, 1987), 137. In another study, J. P. Boulton made comments about popular interest based on a study of Communion tokens issued to tithe-paying parishioners in suburban London. See "The limits of formal religion: the administration of Holy Communion in Late Elizabethan and Early Stuart London," in *The London Journal* 10 (1984): 135–54.

Ages, mostly as a result of the doctrines of the Real Presence and transubstantiation and the offering of Masses for private intentions, those who attended the services would not ordinarily receive the bread and wine. Especially after the death of Henry VIII, new injunctions from the Crown and diocesan authorities insisted on the importance of communicating at least several times a year, if not more often. By 1559, this requirement had been codified in the Prayer Book: "every Parishioner shall communicate, at the leaste thre tymes in the yere, of whiche Easter to be one: and shall also receyve the sacraments."[15] Much has been written about the place of the Holy Communion in early modern popular religion. In a discussion of the Mass as a "social institution," John Bossy notes that there would certainly be "implications . . . drawn by a social historian from the [supersession of the Mass] as the central act of Christian worship."[16] A new understanding of the Communion was essential in order to establish the doctrine of the new church, and as this doctrine developed, attendance at (regular) Communion services was an indicator of orthodoxy. Later, concern about unworthiness to receive the body and blood of Christ, and even apathy, reduced the frequency of the people's communion.[17] The emphasis on popular reception of the communion elements a certain number of times per year surely contributed to the symbolic importance of the ritual as an indicator of religious preference.

The preface to the Order of the Communion prescribes "that the most blessed Sacrament . . . should from thenceforth be commonly delivered and ministered unto all persons within our Realm . . . under both kinds"[18] using the form given by the Crown. The Prayer

[15] *The Prayer-Book of Queen Elizabeth 1559*. Reprint. (Edinburgh: John Grant, 1909), 106.

[16] John Bossy, "The Mass as a Social Institution 1200–1700" in *Past and Present* 100 (August 1983): 30.

[17] See Arnold Hunt, "The Lord's Supper in Early Modern England," in *Past and Present* 161 (November 1998): 39–83.

[18] "The Order of the Communion 1547," in *A Collection of Articles, Injunctions, Canons, Orders, Ordinances, and Constitutions Ecclesiastical, with Other Public Records . . . Chiefly in the Times of K. Edward VIth, Q. Elizabeth, and K. James* (London: Printed by R. Norton for Timothy Garthwait at the Little North-Door

Book of 1559 notes that "the bread and wyne . . . shall be provided by the Curate and the church wardeines, at the charges of the Paryshe, and the paryshe shalbe discharged of suche summes of money."[19] In the Elizabethan *Articles* of 1564, the Communion was to be administered in cathedral churches and colleges "upon the first or second Sunday of every moneth at the least." At these services, "the principal Minister shall use a cope, with gospeller and epistoler agreeably, and at all other prayers to be said at the Communion table, to use no copes but Surplesses."[20] One passage in an early form of the Thirty-Nine Articles of Religion, established in 1552 and intended to "establish the Agreement of true Religion," held that the sacraments "were not ordained of Christ to be Gazed upon, or to be carried about, but we should rightly use them. And in such onely, as worthily received the same, they have a wholesome effect and operation."[21]

There had, of course, been other implications of anti-Romanism for public worship. An injunction from Henry VIII in 1538 ordered that devotional images and the candles burned for those devotions should be removed from churches. Christopher Haigh suggests that local parishes removed the candles alone, intending no longer to portray the images as objects of devotion.[22] According to documentary record, there were significant decreases in bequests to parishes for candles, used as a prayer aid, in the counties of Salisbury, Wiltshire, Berkshire, and Dorset.[23]

Another major change came at the accession of Edward VI in 1547. A new set of injunctions forbade shrines, "decking of Images;

---

of St. Paul's Church, 1661). Accessed via Early English Books Online. Henceforth *Articles.*

[19] *The booke of common praier* (London: Richard Jugge and John Cawood, 1559), folio Niiii.

[20] *Articles*, unpaginated, under "Articles for Administration of Prayer and Sacraments."

[21] Ibid., 45.

[22] Christopher Haigh, ed., *The English Reformation Revisited* (Cambridge, UK: Cambridge University Press, 1987), 12.

[23] Andrew D. Brown, *Popular Piety in Late Medieval England: The Diocese of Salisbury 1250–1550*. (Oxford, UK: Clarendon Press, 1995), 226.

offering of Candels" and lights in churches generally, except for two on the high altar ("for the Sacrament"), "nor [should the parish] allure the people by any inticements, to the Pilgrimage of any Saint or Image." Both images and lights were to be fully removed, "so that there remain no memory of the same in walls, glasses, windows, or elsewhere."[24] The Protestant contention was that the veneration of images constituted idolatry, while the Catholic interpretation saw representations of the saints as inspirational examples of virtuous living.[25] By the same proclamation, Masses said in chantries for the souls of the dead were to be suppressed; instead, "the sacraments [should] be duly, and reverently ministered in . . . Parishes." Importantly, the text demanded that the people should "keep their holy day . . . in often times receiving the Communion, of the very body and blood of Christ."[26] Perhaps in aid of the ministers who were now obliged to preach several times yearly, an English Bible, a government-endorsed "book of homilies" approved by church authorities, and the interpretative *Paraphrases* of Erasmus were to be purchased by each parish.[27]

In 1549, the Act of Uniformity enshrined the new Book of Common Prayer as the authorized reference for worship in churches. The Privy Council ordained that an inventory of the contents of each church should be taken.[28] This order for an inventory was repeated in 1552. By 1550, bishops, including Nicholas Ridley of London, had composed injunctions ordering the wardens to destroy high altars and replace them with "an honest table decently covered" for the distribution of the Communion; since "the forme

[24] *Injunctions* of Edward VI, in *Articles*, 5.

[25] Horton Davies, *Worship and Theology in England* (Grand Rapids, MI: Eerdmans, 1996), 1:352. He notes the Catholic view was supported by the "King's Book" (1534), whose full title is *A necessary Doctrine and erudition for any christen man, set forth by the Kynges maiesty of Englande & c*, and was apparently approved by its eponym.

[26] *Injunctions* of Edward VI in *Articles*, 1–11.

[27] Hutton in Haigh, *English Reformation Revisited*, 124.

[28] Ibid., 125–26.

of a table may more move and tourney the simple frome the olde superstitious opinions of the Popish masse."[29]

The Injunctions of Elizabeth I (1559) repeat many of the Edwardian orders, including that each parish should have a copy of the New Testament in Latin and English, along with the *Paraphrases*.[30] The churchwardens were to note particularly "the Inventories of Vestments, Copes, and other Ornaments, Plate, Books, and specially of Grayles, Couchers, Legends, Processionals, Manuals, Hymnals Portuelles, and such like."[31] Clerics and academics were to "use and wear such seemly habits, garments, and . . . square caps . . . not thereby meaning to attribute any holiness or special worthiness to the said garments."[32] Of the destruction of altars, these *Injunctions* order that any that had not yet been removed "upon opinion conceived of some other order" should be taken down "by oversight of the Curate of the Church and the Churchwardens . . . wherein no riotous or disordered manner to be used."[33] Another document enacted in 1559 was the renewal of the Act of Uniformity, first promulgated by Edward and then repealed under Mary, "to the great decay of the due honour of God, and discomfort to the professors of the truth of Christs Religion."[34] By 1571, Archbishop Grindal of York had codified the necessities for public worship. Aside from the aforementioned books, a table of Commandments, and a copy of the Canons, his Register requires the wardens of each parish to provide a pulpit, a communion table

[29] Nicholas Ridley, *Iniunctions geven in the Visitation of the Reverende father in God . . .* (London, 1550), article v, *Injunctions* 1550. Altars in chapels had been ordered removed in 1548. See Davies, *Worship and Theology in England*, 1:363. To have been able to *see* the liturgical action seems to have been a priority along with the necessity that the liturgical props (the elements, the table) should have a functional resemblance to the signified (i.e. a loaf instead of a wafer).

[30] *Injunctions* of Elizabeth I, in *Articles*, 68.

[31] Ibid., 74.

[32] Ibid., 73.

[33] *Injunctions* Elizabeth I, 78.

[34] Ibid., 75.

complete with cloth and carpet, chalice, paten, a surplice, and a chest with three locks.[35]

At Ashburton (near Dartmoor in Devon) in 1559, marginal notes in the churchwardens' account book betray a frustrated attitude toward the constant changes in policy and the attendant expenses; several years previous, the old rood-loft in the church had been destroyed, later to be replaced at the expense of 40 shillings. The several lines read:

> The men that thys ordinaunses at fyrst did make
> Dyd not thynke Godis word plase for to take
> For yff they had lokyed well there unto
> [A]bout thys mater had not byn somyche adow
> But nowe the truethe ys cum to the lyghthe
> Thys matter ys put clene to hys flyghthe
> Myche was spent herein & dyd no man good
> And for the love there of the pore lackyd fowd.[36]

By no means do these observations suggest that traditional vestiges were everywhere tolerated. The Protestant aesthetic appreciated the lack of decoration and austerity which eventually came to predominate. An observer might have agreed with Bernard Gilpin that "[the Catholics] come to the Church to feede their eyes,

[35] See John Addy, *The Archdeacon and Ecclesiastical Discipline in Yorkshire 1598–1714: Clergy and the Churchwardens* (York: St. Anthony's Press, 1963), 21.

[36] The men that these ordinances at first did make / Did not think God's word pleasing for to take / For if they had looked well thereunto / About this matter had not been so much ado / But now the truth is come to the light / This matter is put clean to flight / Much was spent herein and did no man good / And for the love thereof the poor lacked food. Transcribed in Alison Hanham, ed., *Churchwardens' Accounts of Ashburton, 1479–1580* (Devon and Cornwall Record Society, 1970), 192. While the phrases may be formulaic, that the accounts refer to authorities in an approving tone might also reflect proclivities: ". . . illustrious prince . . . on earth supreme head of the [C of E] (Ashburton, 1539). But compare the unimpressed tone of the rhyming lines also transcribed here.

and not their soules."[37] There was no inconsiderable Protestantism at the local level in the early years. "Contempt for orthodox Eucharistic doctrine," especially "rayling against the sacrament," was a frequent offence tried in the diocesan court of York, where other evidence suggests a fondness for the old religion.[38] The *certayne litel treaties* of John Veron (pub. 1548) suggest that the Mass is "clean contrary to the scriptures and holy fathers . . . [and is] now by the papists . . . defended to pick poor men's pockets."[39] The scale of the destruction (or defacing) of insular medieval art and manuscripts in this period demonstrates a widespread opposition to Rome.

Ultimately to consider the evidence for local attitudes toward doctrine, we must consider the popular dimension: how did the faithful take to these changes, and how was their understanding of the function of church? It has been proposed that non-churchgoers did not attend Sunday services mostly because it was not the faith in which they were raised and to which they were accustomed.[40] Popular rejection of traditional activities would also mean that the rites had lost their intrinsic value.[41] Francis Clark has suggested that the new liturgies of the Church of England did not hold well with the congregation; "the ordinary estimation," he writes, "of Cranmer's liturgy among both clergy and laity was shown by [its] swift rejection . . . even before any official order had been given."[42] Many, including Eamon Duffy in his important work

[37] Horton Davies, *Worship and Theology in England, Book 1: From Cranmer to Baxter and Fox, 1534–1690* (Grand Rapids: MI, Eerdmans), 355–56.

[38] Arthur Geoffrey Dickens, *The Marian Reaction in the Diocese of York, Part 2: The Laity* (London: St. Anthony's Press, 1957), 5.

[39] John Veron, *Certayne Litel Treaties Set Forth by John Veron . . . for the Erudition and Learning, of the Simple & Ingnorant Peopell* (pamphlet printed by Humfrey Powell, ca. 1548), f. Ai v.

[40] Christoher Haigh, "The Continuity of Catholicism in the English Reformation," *Past & Present* 93 (1981): 37–69, 48.

[41] Haigh (*English Reformation Revisited,* 3) opines that "the simple rituals of village ritual were functional—they apparently worked!"

[42] Francis Clark, *Eucharistic Sacrifice and the Reformation*, 2nd ed. (Oxford, UK: Blackwell, 1967), 201.

The Stripping of the Altars, oppose the view that by the sixteenth century there was a favorable attitude toward the Protestantization of English Christianity.[43]

Modern theologians and liturgists, beset by the problems of their own time, have a tendency to seek an ideal past time where the Christian community exists in ideal conditions, and may, in essence, find what they are looking for: a parish seeking the way forward through the adoption of reform. Equally, revisionists will find evidence to support theories that, whether or not they have intrinsic value, challenge the conventional account.

Luther's Reforms to Doctrine and Theology

Martin Luther's own experience of the pre-Tridentine Catholic Church and many of its challenges was to inspire a need to return to Scripture and to expressions of personal faith by individual Christians, and the centrality of the life, resurrection, and sacramentality of Jesus Christ. Among his central contentions was that Christians were justified (that is, brought into a state of sanctification) by personal faith alone, not through "works," for instance, the works of charity or of service to the church which had been identified as praiseworthy by the doctrines of the medieval church, which had made it possible, for instance, to gain an indulgence (the grant of absolution from sins) by participation in certain rites, or by financing the services of the church by paying for priests' or clerks' stipends; it followed that the payment for services to ease the progress of a deceased Christian through Purgatory was also criticized, and the effectuality of such services as masses for the Dead was questioned.

Luther's famous Ninety-Five Theses (1517) concern themselves particularly with what their author considered to be the doctrinal errors of the church. A number of these relate to public worship through the denial that human works (i.e., payment for remission of sins through indulgences) could have a positive effect on salvation. Luther particularly held that the authority of the Pope to issue

[43] Duffy, *The Stripping of the Altars*.

absolution to the faithful was limited to "those [penalties] which he has imposed either by his own authority or by that of the Canons" (thesis 5). Furthermore (thesis 6), "The pope cannot remit any guilt, except by declaring that it has been remitted by God and by assenting to God's remission; though, to be sure, he may grant remission in cases reserved to his judgment. If his right to grant remission in such cases were despised, the guilt would remain entirely unforgiven." He holds as "ignorant and wicked" the practice of reserving canonical penances for purgatory in the case of those who are at the point of death (thesis 10) since (thesis 13) "the dying are freed by death from all penalties; they are already dead to canonical rules, and have a right to be released from them." Anyone, then, who preaches the need for indulgences, or seeks to encourage the faithful to take up "the pope's indulgences" is entirely in error (thesis 21), and those who take them up, similarly, "will be condemned eternally, together with their teachers, who believe themselves sure of their salvation because they have letters of pardon" (thesis 33), given that these "graces of pardon concern only the penalties of sacramental satisfaction, and these are appointed by man" (thesis 34).

Rather than allowing absolution to be purchased, it was necessary for the penitent to be truly repentant: "They preach no Christian doctrine who teach that contrition is not necessary in those who intend to buy souls out of purgatory or to buy confessionalia" (thesis 35); moreover, "every truly repentant Christian has a right to full remission of penalty and guilt, even without letters of pardon" (thesis 36). Not only was it ineffective to buy pardons for oneself, it was not praiseworthy to do it for others (thesis 42): one was "to be taught that the pope does not intend the buying of pardons to be compared in any way to works of mercy"; it was far better to give to the poor or needy (thesis 43). Luther alludes to ritual in a further statement (thesis 55), in a context that is intended to emphasize the supremacy of the Gospel over man-made doctrines and rituals: "It must be the intention of the pope that if pardons, which are a very small thing, are celebrated with one bell, with single processions and ceremonies, then the Gospel, which is the very greatest thing, should be preached with a hundred bells, a hundred processions, a hundred ceremonies."

Luther's theology and arguments had a very significant effect on both the form and the product of public worship. In the Augsburg Confession, the first and most important expression of doctrine of the Lutheran movement, the number of sacraments was made quite clear (three), but the discourse suggests that all those things which have God's command and promise could be thought of as sacraments as well. Of the three central sacraments, baptism (including infant baptism) was necessary and a means of grace, to which children were to be brought in order that God may grant them faith. The body and blood of Christ were truly present in the bread and wine of the Eucharist, which was to be divided and received as another means of grace. Finally, private penance was to be retained. On the basis that sacraments ought to have been instituted by Christ, Luther held there to be three sacraments, baptism, penance, and "the bread," although it could also be said that Christ himself is the principal sacrament, "but with three sacramental signs,"[44] and ultimately, Luther wrote, baptism and the Eucharist ought to be all-satisfying.

Luther's pen did not neglect criticism of the particular form of worship, particularly of the Mass. Liturgy appears to have been for Luther a clear indicator of doctrine, and also a way of identifying corruptions and the means by which they could be ameliorated. In his work *The Abomination of the Secret Mass*, he attacks the wording that suggests that the priest, in the Eucharist, offers up Christ at the altar, arguing that Christ's sacrifice was made once for the sins of all, rather than piecemeal in innumerable individual masses for hundreds of years. "They thereby deny," Luther writes, "both with their deeds and in their hearts, that Christ has washed sin away and has died and risen again. . . . The blasphemy is so great that it must simply wait for eternal hell-fire." He further identifies as a mockery the notion that the priest should be a sort of mediator between God and Christ. Furthermore and pertinently for his attack on prayer for the dead, Luther mocks those who "[pray] for those who repose in the sleep of peace and rest in Christ and have the

[44] Martin Luther, *The Babylonian Captivity of the Church*, trans. A.T.W. Steinhauser, Frederick C. Ahrens, and Abdel Ross Wentz, in *Luther's Works* 36 (Philadelphia: Muhlenberg Press, 1959), 123–25.

sign of faith. If that is true, why should you pray for them? Are you not a madman and a fool?"[45] The so-called Sacrifice of the Mass was certainly never intended to be "turned into mere merchandise, a market, and a profit-making business" which Luther implies it had done in the pre-Tridentine Catholic Church.[46]

Nevertheless, Luther to the last believed in the Real Presence of Christ in the Eucharist, and in the Augsburg Confession the Lutheran reformers argued, in response to claims that their churches had "abolished" the Mass, that it was still "celebrated with the greatest reverence. Almost all the customary ceremonies are also retained, except that German hymns are interspersed here and there among the parts sung in Latin."[47] Nevertheless, Luther very clearly wished to expunge the elements of the Roman Mass most odious to him, especially from the offertory onward. The "words of life and salvation" (the consecration of bread and wine) were lost in a muddle of sacrificial language which, on the logic described above, it was necessary to resolve.[48] Similarly, attention was distracted from the arguments about the efficacy of and the presence of Christ within the sacrament. Instead of invoking Aristotle and philosophical principles, "why do we not put aside such curiosity," Luther wrote, "and cling simply to the words of Christ, willing to remain in ignorance . . . content that the real body of Christ is present by virtue of the words?"[49] He pointed to the Scripturally-attested example of the Last Supper, pointing out that Christ's blessing, breaking, and giving of bread and wine were "most simple, without any display of vestments, gestures, chants, or other ceremonies, so that if it had been necessary to offer the mass as a sacrifice, then Christ's institution of it was not complete." The closer the Mass to the form of the Last Supper, argued Luther, the better to convey the true grace of the sacrament.

[45] Martin Luther, *The Abomination of the Secret Mass,* trans. Abdel Ross Wentz, in *Luther's Works* 36, 322.

[46] Martin Luther, *Babylonian Captivity*, 35.

[47] Article XXIV of the Augsburg Confession.

[48] Martin Luther, *Formula Misse* in PEER, 191.

[49] Martin Luther, *Babylonian Captivity*, 33.

Zwingli and Calvin

While Martin Luther may have been offering a revised version with some fundamental changes of the liturgical forms and theology he hoped to influence in another direction, the Swiss pastor Ulrich Zwingli (d. 1531) had a very different idea of sacramentality: "If your faith is not so perfect as not to need a ceremonial sign to confirm it, it is not faith."[50] Such signs should not, in the Zwinglian tradition, transmit anything but a remembrance. Sacraments, comprising only baptism and "the Lord's Supper," were to have some sort of "initiatory function," the first to conform to the rule of Christ in life, and the second to trust in the death of Christ and thanksgiving for the blessing of redemption through that death. All other sacraments were merely "ceremonials." John Calvin (d. 1564), by contrast, held that the sacraments were effective because God "executes what ever he promises and represents in signs; nor do the signs lack their own effect in proving their Author truthful and faithful." Received with the Spirit and with true faith, they had "the same office as the Word of God," namely to bring Christ and his grace to the faithful.[51]

Both Zwingli and Calvin, along with Luther, ascribed importance to infant baptism in reaction to the belief of the Anabaptists, articulated by Menno Simons, that "baptism cannot be administered to [young children] without perverting the ordinance of the Lord."[52] Zwingli believed that baptism was "simply a mark or pledge by which those who receive it are dedicated to God."[53] Calvin held it to be a "token and proof of our cleansing" as well as a witnessing to Christ and religion in the world.[54]

[50] Ulrich Zwingli, *Commentary on True and False Religion*, trans. S.M. Jackson and C.N. Heller (Durham, NC: Labyrinth Press, 1981), 184.

[51] John Calvin, *Institutes of the Christian Religion* IV, trans. Ford Lewis Battles, in *Library of Christian Classics* 21 (London: SCM Press, 1961), chapter 14.

[52] Menno Simons, "Foundation of Christian Doctrine," trans. Leonard Verduin, in *The Complete Writings of Menno Simons* (Scottdale, PA: Herald Press, 1956), 120.

[53] Ulrich Zwingli, *Of Baptism*, trans. G.W. Bromiley, in *Library of Christian Classics* 24 (London: SCM Press, 1953), 145.

[54] John Calvin, *Institutes* IV, in *Library of Christian Classics* 21, chapter 15, 1303.

The Eucharistic theology of Zwingli and Calvin, too, differed considerably from Luther's. For Zwingli, in the words of institution "This is my body," "the word "is" is not to be taken literally," giving as a comparable statement a wife introducing her late husband's wedding ring as her husband himself. He denies completely the argument of the Real Presence of Christ in the Eucharist, to say nothing of transubstantiation. Calvin's argumentation is more subtle: the worthy receiver of the bread and wine takes it "not . . . solely by imagination or understanding of mind, but to enjoy the thing itself as nourishment of eternal life." He states clearly, however, that "Unless the body of Christ can be everywhere at once, without limitation of place, it will not be credible that he lies hidden under the bread in the Supper."[55]

Doctrinal Continuity and Change at the Council of Trent

The function of this ecumenical council was not only to address some of the questions and dissent raised by the Protestant reformers, but also to give careful consideration to the criticisms of certain abuses of doctrine and worship that had been reported in the church. In many cases the canons of Trent appear to be doing both at once. Canons of the Seventh Session of the council establish clearly the number of the sacraments (seven), all with equal validity, and the fact they were all established by Jesus Christ. The council held that the sacraments are necessary for salvation, though not all may be experienced by all Christians (notably marriage and holy orders). Luther's proposition of justification by faith alone without the sacraments is soundly refuted, and equally it was clear that faith alone was not the cause of grace (as if the sacraments were merely outward signs of grace received through faith); rather, the grace conferred was understood to have been conveyed through the performance of the sacramental act. Similarly the sacraments were not instituted for the nourishment of faith alone.

As for particular sacraments, the council agreed that infant baptism was efficacious and that baptism (or rebaptism) at the age of

[55] John Calvin, *Institutes* IV, chapter 7.30.

reason was not, and that confirmation was also valid, and not a mere process of catechesis. Each celebration of the Mass was a real sacrifice offered to God, which could be offered for persons present or absent, living or dead, and Masses said by a priest with no other communicants were wholly valid. The Real Presence of Christ in the Eucharist was completely affirmed for any part of both the bread and wine, however small, and any purely symbolic interpretation deprecated; furthermore, the doctrine of transubstantiation (and the word denoting it) were entirely valid. It was also reaffirmed that the laity and noncelebrating clergy should not receive the wine (again in response to queries from the reformers about communicating under both species). The Canon of the Mass was to be retained, and the entire service carried out in Latin, and the ceremonial elements which the reformers argued were distracting and impious were to be commended. In sum, while Trent rationalized Mass and Office, the notable conservatism of the changes in the liturgy demonstrates that most liturgical and sacramental doctrines did not change substantially.

In July 1570, Pius V promulgated a new Roman Missal, which for the most part remained the normative form of service until the 1960s. This liturgical monument, which accurately reflected the theological position of the church in the late sixteenth century, exemplifies how forms of worship can both illustrate and uphold a doctrinal position which, in this case, was not reevaluated seriously until the twentieth century.

The Doctrines of the New Church of England

In response to the doctrines promulgated by the Council of Trent, and with a view to contradicting many of its key arguments, the Church of England issued its Articles of Religion in 1563. These Articles, included with the text of subsequent editions of the Book of Common Prayer, were the definitive expression of faith, agreement with which was required of all clergy and, indeed, those teaching or learning in the universities of Oxford and Cambridge, and in other positions of authority, until the nineteenth century. Despite the fact that some of the principles expounded in the Articles were—some even after their promulgation—now habitually unheeded (for instance, the rule against the reservation of the Sacrament), they remained and still remain, at least in name, part of the governing doctrine of the Church of England. As might be expected, the purpose, efficacy, and forms of worship are discussed at length, together with some of their theological foundations.

Article XXIV establishes clearly, in contradiction of the Roman practice and, in fact, of the earliest worship of the independent Church of England, that "it is a thing plainly repugnant to the word of God and the custom of the primitive Church, to have public prayer in the Church, or to minister the sacraments in a tongue not understanded of the people." In response to the Zwinglian comment that sacraments are "tokens," and also to the Tridentine affirmation of the *status quo*, Article XXV identifies sacraments:

> ordained of Christ [as] not only badges or tokens of Christian men's profession, but rather they be certain sure witnesses and effectual signs of grace and God's good will toward us, by the which He doth work invisibly in us, and doth not only quicken, but also strengthen and confirm, our faith in Him. There are two Sacraments ordained of Christ our Lord in the Gospel, that is to say, Baptism and the Supper of the Lord. Those five commonly called Sacraments, that is to say, Confirmation, Penance, Orders, Matrimony, and Extreme Unction, are not to be counted for Sacraments of the Gospel, being such as have grown partly of the corrupt following of the Apostles, partly are states of life allowed in the Scriptures; but yet have not the like nature of Sacraments with Baptism and the Lord's Supper, for that they have not any visible sign or ceremony ordained of God.

Notably, and despite the high opinion of the "Sacraments ordained of Christ," the same article continues:

> The Sacraments were not ordained of Christ to be gazed upon or to be carried about, but that we should duly use them. And in such only as worthily receive the same, have they a wholesome effect or operation: but they that receive them unworthily, purchase to themselves damnation, as Saint Paul saith.

The approach to the "Lord's Supper" takes a similar line to that of the other reformers: it is a "partaking" in the body and blood of

Christ, "not only a sign of the love that Christians ought to have among themselves, one to another, but rather it is a sacrament of our redemption by Christ's death," but transubstantiation is:

> repugnant to the plain words of Scripture, overthroweth the nature of a Sacrament, and hath given occasion to many superstitions. The body of Christ is given, taken, and eaten in the Supper, only after an heavenly and spiritual manner. And the mean whereby the body of Christ is received and eaten in the Supper is Faith. (article XXVIII)

Finally, it is clearly indicated, reiterating an earlier point that the consecrated bread and wine were not in any way to be "reserved, carried about, lifted up, or worshipped," an obvious reference to the practices of the Roman Church. Similarly (article XXII)

> The Romish doctrine concerning Purgatory, Pardons, worshipping and adoration as well of Images as of Relics, and also Invocation of Saints, is a fond thing vainly invented, and grounded upon no warranty of Scripture; but rather repugnant to the word of God.

In a time of great theological and cultural upheaval, as well as the perceived threat of Catholic influence (which can be seen very clearly in the ways that some apparently Catholic practices were portrayed), the Thirty-Nine Articles offered a clear expression of the faith of the Church of England, especially as it was reflected in forms of worship and devotion.

THE AGE OF PRINT

By the time of the pan-European and wider-reaching activities of the Protestant reformers, the craft of printing had advanced very considerably in reach and quality, and printed service books were rapidly replacing hand-written manuscript copies. Printing also greatly ameliorated the accurate, wide-scale, rapid transmission of written ideas over large geographical areas, allowing the fruits of intellectual discourse to be widely disseminated. It was also possible for the first time through printing to produce a very large number of service books with more or less identical contents, allowing for the wholesale standardization of rites that had, by virtue of local variation and the necessarily unique products of copying an exemplar by hand, never been made uniform. Printing made possible the promulgation of the fixed form of the Tridentine Missal and the Book of Common Prayer, as well as all the other printed rites, in their diversity, produced by the reformers.

The emergence of printed books for worship and prayer in large numbers meant that it was possible (and increasingly economical), for more than the few persons actually conducting the service to have a copy of the text. For liturgies in Latin, this would have aided the comprehension of Latin-literate persons who also possessed a book. But it also meant that, if the rites were in the vernacular, people would be able to read and follow the form of service for themselves, rather than listening or being prayerfully present while not following the precise form of the service. The forms of worship, then, took on the function of edifying the people and providing them with a spiritual resource that, even if they did not contribute outwardly to it, was beneficial to their inward actions.

In England, when the first surviving Primer (devotional book) with principal contents in English was printed in 1534, it was one of a very few books in the vernacular whose texts were based on Scripture. Interestingly enough under Catholic Queen Mary, the Primer was one of the few books containing Scripture in the vernacular to be permitted.[56]

Whether or not their owners used the books to pray during or around public services, and whether they understood fully what they were saying, cannot be answered adequately, but what is clear is that over time, and beginning with manuscript copies, Books of Hours and Primers contained an increasing number of prayers, devotions, and directions in English. This seems to represent an acknowledgment of readers who were literate in the vernacular. The existence of Hours and Primers in these circumstances suggests that they should be important sources for the role of the vernacular in private devotional life. Bibliographical records suggest

[56] Charles C. Butterworth, *The English Primers (1529–1545): Their Publication and Connection with the English Bible and the Reformation in England* (Philadelphia: University of Pennsylvania Press, 1953), 2.

that Primers were in comparatively higher demand after the principal contents, the Hours of the Virgin, had been translated into English. In a book-trade which had always been international in scope, it is significant that a high proportion of these later English editions were produced domestically.

Eamon Duffy makes the notable comment that Richard Pynson, one of the early London printers, believed himself part of the catechetical movement.[57] Mary Erler goes somewhat further in suggesting that deliberate replacement of Latin with English "suggests the importance of the printer's role both in responding to social change *and in bringing it about*."[58] Both Duffy and Erler seem to suggest that rather than being "passive" participants in the development of literacy, the printers were quite engaged with it.

THE VERNACULAR

The Thirty-Nine Articles of the Church of England provide a very clear statement that public services should be held in a language understood by the laity, and similar principles were eventually followed by most of the reformers. But this was not always a universally favored decision. In the initial deliberations of the English bishops about new forms of service to be developed, Archbishop Cranmer argued that English should be used "except in certain mysteries, whereof I doubt." He was joined by Nicholas Ridley, bishop of London, who stated that Mass should be said in English except the Consecration, which was to be said in silence. Bishop Tunstall of Durham countered that Latin should be used primarily since it united all Western Christians, but "certain prayers might be in the mother tongue, for the instruction and stirring of the devotion of the people."[59] The consensus being against a fully vernacular service, the form of the "Order of the Communion" (1548) was adopted, which provided that the priest need not always

[57] Duffy, *The Stripping of the Altars*, 83.

[58] Mary Erler, "*The Maner to Lyue Well* and the Coming of English in Francois Regnault's Primers of the 1520s and 1530s," *The Library*, 6th ser. vi (1984), 243. Emphasis mine.

[59] In *Order of the Communion 1548*, ed. H.A. Wilson (London, 1908), xiv.

give communion to the people, but should do so on such days as he has previously announced, with an exhortation encouraging them to prepare to receive the Sacrament. The rite as printed provides for the form of the exhortation, in English, a general confession (spoken by the priest in the name of all present) and absolution, as well as the "Comfortable Words" (Come to me, all ye that labor, etc.), and "We do not presume" (said by the priest alone) and finally the words of administration.

Foundations of Methodism

The Methodist Church was founded by John and Charles Wesley, first as a movement within the Church of England with its origins in Oxford. The term "Methodist" derives from the systematic approach to rigorous Christian life of the founders, who set aside large quantities of time for worship, private prayer, study, and acts of charity. Methodism expanded into many local groups which, after John Wesley began ordaining ministers and particularly after his death, grew into a number of churches independent from Anglican authority. John Wesley saw the Prayer Book and the worship of the Church of England, as well as much of its sacramental theology, as a starting point for the worship of his own congregations, and his brother Charles was responsible for writing a very large quantity of hymns which, prized for their elegance and sentiment, have remained vital to Christian worship ever since.

⁘ ⁘ ⁘

Every one of the new Christian identities forged by the reformers saw worship as an important concern requiring careful consideration. The contrasting approaches of Luther and Calvin to the liturgy illustrated the differences between their respective theologies. Despite nods to the vernacular that antedate the break with Rome, Henry VIII's Church of England was in no immediate hurry to distance itself from the liturgy of the past, except where it was carried out by dissolved monasteries. The debates over Anglican faith and doctrine, when they did happen, produced a Prayer Book which in its various editions reflected the continuities and changes from earlier practice. Methodism stressed its continuity with Anglican worship until theological rifts caused the movement to split in various directions, the descendant churches desirous for worship that reflected their own identities. The Tridentine consolidation of the liturgy generated patterns for worship that did not change until the mid-twentieth century, and it was only then, too, that congregations were able to understand these patterns. In all of these cases, at a time when heterogeneity appeared permanently for the first time in the worship and doctrine of the Western church, the liturgy also afforded lay people the opportunity to experience the reflexive relationship between learning and remembering their faith.

CHAPTER 4

The Later Middle Ages

The helmsman sent from Heaven, at the stern,
seemed to have blessedness inscribed upon him;
more than a hundred spirits sat within.
"In exitu Isräel de Aegypto,"
with what is written after of that psalm,
all of those spirits sang as with one voice.
—*Dante Alighieri,* The Divine Comedy[1]

The liturgical practices and motivations of Christians in the Middle Ages, as well as the intellectual backdrop that influenced them, are all very well attested in literature, in historical sources, and in the vast and well-presented collection of material artefacts of the period, including art, manuscripts, architecture, and church furnishings. Many European countries boast a continuity of religious activity from the present back to the period in the high and late Middle Ages, where worship scaled as yet unsurpassed heights of centrality, complexity, and elaboration. Parish churches, cathedrals, and museums of the present delight in showcasing artefacts used in worship which are recognizable and sometimes even still in use, even if their return to functionality may be a product of the Romantic rediscovery of the ancient past described in chapter 2.

All this apparently available evidence of medieval Christianity means that at first mention, it seems as if we know a great deal

[1] Dante Alighieri, *The Divine Comedy*, trans. Allen Mandelbaum (London: Everyman's Library, 1995), *Purgatorio* II, vv. 43–48 (p. 222).

about the religion of the Middle Ages, mediated by interest in its liturgical texts and music, by the surviving material evidence, and by the extensive and sometimes profligate interest in liturgy and matters of church in literary works. For at least the past one hundred fifty years, there has been an outpouring of academic interest in the philological project of establishing the texts and music of the medieval liturgy. This outpouring comes partly out of the Romantic desire to restore the trappings of the past, motivated by the belief that medieval forms of service as well as their accoutrements were successful in inspiring piety and devotion. It comes partly out of the nineteenth century's more general obsession with the redaction of ancient texts.

The liturgical music of the Middle Ages, being the origin of polyphonic music and a direct antecedent of all subsequent sacred genres, not to mention the backbone of the Western musical tradition, has enjoyed a great deal of interest and awareness over the past two centuries. The survival of the fabric of medieval churches, albeit in altered form in most cases, and the continued use of many of these buildings for an unaltered purpose, unites worshipping Christians of today with their medieval forebears, and helps them identify with worshippers of the past, even if that connection is made primarily through a recognition of how different the lives of medieval Christians must have been.

As historical sites, too, we are drawn to medieval churches as buildings that are more than tourist locations. We imagine how they were used by their original inhabitants and are often aided by richly illustrated historical and archaeological interpretative guides through which we can measure the lives of medieval Christians against our own, especially the lives of those clergy and religious who inhabited cathedrals, abbeys, and collegiate churches whose rules of life and habitual patterns of worship are well documented. In museums, too, we can readily equate many of the medieval church artefacts with understandable practices. Even if the veneration of relics and solemn processions of the Blessed Sacrament of Christ's body and blood do not now enjoy universal popularity, such practices continue to thrive in many places, and are normative in Catholic communities. Similarly, it is possible to imagine celebrations commemorating the life or death of saints because such practices continue to exist widely: visitors to Spain, for instance, will encounter processions in honor of the Blessed Virgin Mary which lack nothing compared with their medieval antecedents. In Britain and America, the widespread and ongoing interest in the Tudor period (at least in part inspired by school history lessons which mean it is one period of history known to most), as well as the existence of the Church of England, its historical forms of worship and indeed the mythologies of that institution's foundation, point out the disparities between Catholic and Protestant theology and liturgical priorities, again forging a link through disparity between present and historical practice.

We are also the inheritors of the literary output of the Middle Ages which, in its subjects, but also more implicitly in the way it appropriates liturgical texts and themes, quite understandably emphasizes the central role of worship in Christian life. But it also betrays familiarity with textual forms and theological precepts. Chaucer's pilgrims, Dante's inhabitants of the afterlife, and the colorful characters of liturgical and civic drama are all literary voices for whom worship held a central place in life (and death).

In the late Middle Ages (broadly speaking from the fourteenth to the sixteenth centuries), an era where fixed forms of liturgical practice were being carefully created, learnt, and often well recorded, public worship was the authentic, authorized, public expression of the church in the world, inseparable from all aspects of life. Echoes of the liturgy are discernible in innumerable contemporary witnesses which demonstrate the extent to which its prose, poetry, music, and ceremonial permeated medieval thought, action, and expression. The liturgy was rooted in the temporal cycles of day and year, and influenced in part by the cycles of agriculture. Consequently, it governed ordinary routine as well as major life events such as birth, marriage, and death. As the principal means by which the church interacted with its people and provided an important means of grace through which they were sanctified, the liturgy influenced popular devotion and personal attitudes to religion and spirituality as well as politics, making it a concern for authorities, rebels, and reformers. In addition, it was the source of all sacred music and patron of some of the period's greatest art and architecture. The surviving books of the liturgy constitute a significant proportion of the books extant from the Middle Ages. Each was the result of considerable effort and attention.

It is, therefore, difficult to speak of liturgy and worship as a self-contained subject of consideration in the Middle Ages. The available critical material, except for introductory guides and reference material, tends to deal with very specific topics. It is also challenging for us to disconnect our own views and understandings of medieval worship. These views are often the product of historical teaching, as well as our own interactions with texts, music, art, architecture, and literary depictions of the liturgy of the Middle Ages. Our received view often differs from the rather more complex picture that emerges if the surviving evidence is carefully reassessed.

This chapter therefore begins with an interrogation of the functionality of late medieval worship. We will explore some of the key categories of liturgical practice, how they were understood by intellectuals, and how they were experienced by the laity. We will spend some time examining the historical and theological background of liturgical practice, and will consider the Office of the Dead in detail as an observance which highlights some of the theological and experiential conclusions which can be made.

WHY WORSHIP?

As well as being the central outward expression of the life of the church and the principal occupation of clerics of all orders, the liturgy of the later Middle Ages was, for those who were not actively involved in carrying it out, a focal point for personal prayer and devotion which was carried out in the presence of, and guided by the context, imagery, allusions, and sensory stimuli of the liturgical ceremonies being performed. In common with that of other historical periods, the liturgy of the late Middle Ages was a powerful social and theological tool with near-universal reach and cultural resonance, and very much the expression of the life of the church that clerics and laity alike were able to internalize, and by which they defined their own faith and devotion.

The rites themselves were marked by great expansion of earlier forms, greater complexity of tasks to be performed, and elaboration of existing genres. This led to a plurality of traditions across medieval Europe and in different types of religious institutions. These complicated rites were performed by an increasingly professionalized body of clerics, mostly to the exclusion of lay congregations from what a later generation would call "active participation," meaning there was a considerable division between clerical and lay experience of the same services.

Notwithstanding this sequestration of lay experience outside the privileged domain of authorized text in favor of self-directed interaction through private devotion, liturgy was truly a feast for all the senses. It was carried out in buildings designed to reflect on the central theological principles that also determined the form of worship, and the liturgical features that could be sensed by the laity outside the choir served to focus their own private prayers. Worship was experienced by material beings attuned to the material senses: the movement of processions and bells at the consecration helped to attract attention; incense recalled the vision of Isaiah the prophet; the cool, tooled surfaces of chalice and paten during the Eucharist were touched by few, but many knew the discomfort of standing or kneeling in a furniture-less nave throughout long services. Some—but not all—would feel the touch of the host on their tongues, the touch of the sacrament.

The Daily Round of Worship

In the later Middle Ages, the schedule of daily public worship was at its fullest, and the rites at their most complicated and professionalized. In addition to the main Mass of the day in a church or other ecclesiastical institution, celebrated by the priest (or duty priest in a larger community), any additional clergy would celebrate additional Masses, many of which were for special intentions (i.e., intended for the spiritual benefit of a person, living or deceased, or for a particular wish) or using a form particularly dedicated to Jesus or to Mary, or to a saint. In religious communities mainly comprised of priests, these additional Masses not only fulfilled the obligation of the clergy—dating from the eleventh century onward—to celebrate the Eucharist daily whenever possible (even in religious communities mainly comprised of priests), but also satisfied the requirements of certain benefactions to churches, usually by wealthy individuals in which a chaplain was hired and supported in order to say Mass and Office for the repose of the soul of some deceased person in Purgatory. This practice, very frequent in this period, was often the cause of the expansion of the number of clergy in ecclesiastical institutions.

During these additional Masses, the priest would normally not be joined by any assisting clerics or lay people, but would instead recite the service by himself; the offering of the Mass was understood to have been made by the priest on behalf of the sponsor of the services, that is, the benefactor whose gift allowed the service to take place. Many churches had more than one altar, each dedicated to a particular saint, and these additional altars were brought into regular service for Masses with special intentions. Such "sponsored" services were undertaken for the sponsor's spiritual benefit whether or not he or she was present (or living). Yet in these circumstances the sponsor (even if deceased) was, spiritually speaking, fulfilling a similar role to a lay person hearing a Mass offered by the celebrant on behalf of the Christian community. To endow the daily celebration of Mass was, spiritually speaking, just as efficacious as being present oneself, since in neither case would a lay person take a more obviously active role. It was not customary for the laity to receive any of the consecrated bread or wine, and unlike that of the absent sponsor, the lay spiritual reward of grace was conveyed by attendance.

Although the significance of attending services was well understood and the spiritual benefits well communicated, it was not unusual for most persons attending a service to be unaware of the particular texts said or actions carried out at the altar. Even at the principal Mass of the day in a community of clerics (for instance a monastery) the action at the altar and the chanted texts intoned by the choir or community would not necessarily have aligned at many of the right points, sometimes competing to be heard, and often it was only the assistant ministers near the altar who would have heard a great deal of what the celebrant was saying. Beyond some of the readings, prayers, some of the Eucharistic Prayer, and some of the verses and responses exchanged between the celebrant and the choir, little of what was said at the altar was audible from the choir, let alone from further away. Of the choir's contribution, the chanted Introit, Gradual, Alleluya and sequence, Offertory, and Communion were all settings of texts which, like the readings, changed from celebration to celebration, whereas the "Ordinary" of the Mass, namely the Kyrie eleison (*Lord, have mercy*, a cry for deliverance), Gloria in excelsis deo (*Glory to God in the highest*, praise to God), Credo in unum Deum (*I believe in one God*, a statement of faith), Sanctus and Benedictus (*Holy, holy, holy* and *Blessed is he*, both adoration of God), and Agnus Dei (*Lamb of God*, a prayer for mercy and peace) remained constant features, although according to custom they were sung to different melodies at different times. All of these sung items were necessarily the main contribution of the choir or community to the service, and left little time for engaging with what might have been happening at the altar, even if it had been audible. A considerable proportion of the priest's text of the Mass was said even before exiting the sacristy and entering the church, and only a minority of the priest's part was spoken when the choir was silent, which made the choir's contribution even more important for the lay experience of the Mass.

In addition to the Mass was the now well-established eightfold round of daily prayer. The liturgical day began with Vespers (Evening Prayer), followed by Compline (Night Prayer) which was sung at nightfall. Early the next morning the cycle continued with Matins (an example showing the complexity and length of this service is given below), Lauds (Morning Prayer) at daybreak, followed by Prime, Terce, Sext, and None (often known as the "little hours" for their brevity and lack of variation) throughout the day at the first, third, sixth, and ninth hours after daybreak. All of these services except Matins followed a broadly similar structure. Each began with an opening dialogue between officiant and choir, followed by the singing of psalms according to a fixed pattern and bookended with short melodies called antiphons. There were passages of Scripture prescribed for short readings as well as canticles, such as Benedictus (the "Song of Zechariah") at Lauds and Magnificat (the "Song of Mary") at Vespers, in addition to subsequent dialogues and prayers. At Matins the service was divided into three (or four in monastic communities) sections called nocturns, each composed of antiphons with psalms, readings, and longer sung items called responsories that usually reflected on some aspect of the readings. The clergy and singers knew all one hundred fifty psalms by heart, as well as the canticles and many other items that remained constant throughout the year, although the antiphons, responsories, and readings were all determined by the day or feast being observed. The late Middle Ages saw a great increase in the number of feast days where the variable items at Mass and Office were specially selected, or in many cases newly written for the purpose. Some of the particularly popular late medieval observances were the feasts of Corpus Christi and the Holy Name of Jesus (both devotions to Christ), and the several feast days in honor of the Virgin Mary, as well as the feast days of recently canonized saints such as Thomas of Canterbury and Anne, mother of Mary. All of these observances had newly-composed liturgical texts and chants written for performance on the correct day of the year, and these proper Offices spread throughout the Western church with remarkable rapidity in the later Middle Ages. In a similar way, some existing texts and chants were expanded or elaborated with new text, giving them a new significance while recalling the original version.

Laity attending the services of the daily Office would have heard dialogues sung by the officiant and choir, psalmody with alternate verses sung by the two sides of the choir—which in larger churches was normally arranged in stalls around a central aisle—and antiphons whose first few words were intoned before the psalmody and canticles, and which were sung in full afterward, as well as short lessons delivered by a reader and prayers and other items intoned by the officiant. There was no opportunity whatever for participation of hearers outside the choir (not dissimilar to Choral Evensong as sung in some institutions), including during items, such as the Our Father, which might have been known to the memories of those attending outside the choir. As for the Mass, it was understood that the offering of clerical worship was presented to God on behalf of the faithful, for whom (if they were attending) it was an opportunity simply to be present in silence while the ceaseless prayer of the church continued around them.

Unrelated to developments in public worship, it was increasingly the case that lay people and clerics alike became attuned to their own personal need for contrition and grace. Much private prayer and devotion, including within the context of public services which they attended, was committed to prayer of a penitential nature, often asking for the intercession of saints. Some such private prayers, said with regularity, gained the faithful certain spiritual favors, many of which related to absolution from sins.

The lives of those who had duties at the altar or in the choir, whether as a priest, a nonordained religious, or as a cleric in lower orders, were substantially determined by the content and the considerably expanded forms of public worship. Their temporal lives were governed by strict rules for the perpetual enactment of Mass and Office. For these persons, another function of worship, in addition to it being part of the corporate offering of prayer and thanksgiving to God, was the enrichment of their own thoughts, prayers, and activities by the Scriptural and spiritual resource found in the texts and chants they performed. Lay people, even if they were literate, had a much less clear understanding of what was happening on the clerical side of the rood-screen, the partition separating choir and nave, and devoted their time spent during church services in support of inward devotion and prayer while interacting with the wider community and with the divine through veneration of the sacrament of the Eucharist.

THE INSTITUTIONAL BACKDROP

Considerable diversity had been the result of the highly regionalized development of liturgical practice as it happened in the West, as will be seen more clearly in the following chapter. It was the Carolingian reforms, beginning in the eighth century, that saw the Roman "Rite"—influenced by the practices of the Franks—replace or substantially overtake the Gallican, Mozarabic, Ambrosian, Beneventan, "Old Roman," Celtic, and other regional rites.

In the later Middle Ages, the liturgical pattern of the papal Curia (employed by the administrators who ran the church in Rome) became an increasingly strong influence on practices elsewhere in its own right. But local and sometimes national independence within the Roman Rite remained in important or influential communities such as Rouen, Paris, and Salisbury. In these places, local "Uses" (variants on the Roman Rite which had their own distinctive characteristics, including choice and order of liturgical texts for the various services) predominated, and sometimes spread. In places like Salisbury or York in England, the local influence went far beyond the eponymous cathedral closes and into much larger areas (in the English case whole ecclesiastical provinces), where the ceremonies and observances proper to the cathedral must have taken on a different, locally determined form.

This localization was probably (for one thing) a result of endowments to ecclesiastical institutions which supplied additional clerics to perform services for particular intentions, devotions, or for the souls of the deceased. In addition to monasteries, cathedrals, and well-endowed parish churches, these supernumerary clerics populated chantry chapels built and endowed for the spiritual service of their patrons, as well as collegiate churches comprised of larger communities of priests. In the larger communities, where canons were appointed on a more or less honorary or nonresidential basis, vicars (from the Latin for "substitute") were appointed to carry out the responsibilities of the canons, including their choral duties. The professionalization of the vicars as liturgical functionaries (and choral singers) in these larger institutions gave rise to a considerable improvement in the institutional capacity to sing more complicated (i.e., polyphonic) music.

The appearance of such secular institutions should not be understood as a diminishment of the importance of the monastic orders. In the later Middle Ages, Benedictine monasticism had reached its height of influence and power both temporally and spiritually (many English cathedrals, for instance, were monastic foundations) and monasteries under the *Rule* of St. Benedict were the most numerous, each with its own distinct, unique, and fixed pattern of liturgical practices, with this independence probably emphasized by the fact that the members of the community lived a life enclosed in the monastery. Exceptions were found in the Cluniac monasteries, which based their customs and liturgy on the mother house at Cluny and whose worship represented a summit of complexity, and the Cistercian houses (founded at Cîteaux) which reacted against the elaboration in liturgy, art, and architecture in favor of simplicity and aesthetic austerity. Others living in communities were described as canons regular (so called because they were members of an ecclesiastical community living under a rule). Many such groups followed the *Rule* of St. Augustine: while Augustinians often used or modified liturgical rites native to the community in which they were situated, Cluniac and Cistercian liturgies followed shared patterns within a common Benedictine inheritance. Nevertheless, it was not necessarily the case that Benedictines of any description, upon visiting another monastery, would automatically have been able to instantly feel liturgically at home.

In the later Middle Ages there also emerged new religious orders of friars including the Franciscans, who drew their inspiration from Francis of Assisi (d. 1226), and the Order of Preachers (Dominicans), founded by St. Dominic (d. 1221). Friars, often known as members of "mendicant" or begging orders, lived in conditions of poverty with no personal possessions, and traveled widely in their work as preachers, scholars, and teachers. Both of these orders made substantial contributions to the contemporaneous internalization of piety and devotion, and the influence of friar-theologians such as St. Thomas Aquinas was felt far beyond the remit of religious communities. Because they traveled frequently, friars' liturgical practices could be much more abbreviated than those of enclosed monks, and rather than relying on community memory (see below) and comprehensive reference volumes, friars' liturgies needed to be recorded in relatively small books: the breviary, a book containing all the necessary texts to say the Office, became an important new type of liturgical book in this period, and a good number of breviaries were travel-sized. Dominicans used a pattern which was standardized across the order by command of Humbert of Romans (d. 1277), Master-General of the order, while Franciscans used a modified version of the Use of the Roman Curia.

For all members of religious orders, the liturgy occupied a large and central proportion of the day's (and night's) work, around which their other obligations to work and study were arranged. The Benedictine aphorism "Nothing is to be preferred to the work of God" illustrates the mutual dependence of monasteries on the liturgy and vice versa. For friars and others who traveled alone or in small groups, regular worship was also a link with their fellow religious, scattered in friaries or living in larger communities, as well as a means of stabilizing sometimes uncertain or unfamiliar living conditions and employment with familiar forms of worship and prayer, held in common with other members of the order. Both the mendicant orders and those who lived together in community were very influential in the development of supra-regional liturgical patterns which interacted with the secular Uses that were developing on a diocesan or local basis. It was this amalgam of different traditions, mainly distinguished by the choice and order of sung texts and readings and by various distinctive ceremonial practices, which contributed to the growth, in great diversity, to the liturgical experience of the late medieval Western Christian. Some insight into the lay experience of religious life comes in a moral treatise of Petrarch (d.1374), *On Religious Leisure*. He recalls a visit to his brother, a Benedictine monk:

> While I wondered at your devoted silence and angelic singing, while I admired you, all together at times and at times individually . . . the whole brief time fled by me without my realizing it. . . . Why should I say more? Thus it happened that I departed, almost in silence, intent and gaping in wonder at everyone and looking around at everything, hearing words on all sides and saying things in bits and pieces . . . Now finally having returned to my own solitude and mindful of that whole blessed sweetness which I drank in with you, our Lord's bees, a well-born race, and now, thinking over the experience in private, I find many things of long-term benefit which that all-too-brief stay has given to me.[2]

[2] Francesco Petrarca, *On Religious Leisure (De otio religioso)*, ed. and trans. Susan S. Schearer (New York: Italica Press, 2002), 4.

Many of the distinctions from tradition to tradition within the monastic world would have been entirely opaque to the ordinary lay attendee, but the rich regional distinctiveness of worship was the stimulus for extensive local artistic and ceremonial expressions such as music, processions, and architecture, which were themselves represented in literary and historical writings.

THE MEDIEVAL THEOLOGY OF WORSHIP AND THE SACRAMENTS

As much as the daily round of public prayer occupied the majority of time for clergy and religious, the lives of all Christians were governed and sanctified by the sacraments of the church, many of which took place in the context of worship, and it was their understanding of the function of the sacraments which inspired much of their own active prayer and devotional activities. Much scholarly effort was expended in the later Middle Ages to establish a sophisticated understanding of the underlying principles behind the seven sacraments (baptism, confirmation, penance, Eucharist, marriage, ordination, anointing of the sick), the conditions in which they should be celebrated, and the potential problems which could arise. These deliberations were addressed by scholastic theologians and ecclesiastical bodies rather than in a public or popular forum, but the understanding of the rites as expounded by these theologians had a considerable influence on how the faithful interacted with the sacramental life of their church. Aside from the daily round of public worship and prayer practiced almost exclusively by clergy and religious and in ecclesiastical institutions, and the occasional sacraments which served to sanctify critical life events of the faithful, there was an ever-greater emphasis on the celebration of the Eucharist, the principal sacrament by which Christ's own body and blood were made present in the world.

The fifteenth-century Council of Florence established that the seven Christian sacraments, unlike the sacraments of the Jewish law, "truly contain grace and confer it on those who worthily receive it." The council established the sevenfold pattern of the life of the church through the sacraments: Christians experience rebirth through baptism; strengthening through confirmation; nourishment through the Eucharist; recovery from sin through penance; healing through the sacrament of the sick; and the church is governed by orders and expanded through marriage.[3] Of all the sacraments, Hugh of St. Victor (circa 1140) supplies a working definition thus: "A sacrament is a corporeal or material element set before the senses without, representing by similitude and signifying by institution and containing by sanctification some invisible and spiritual grace."[4] The material nature of the sacrament, then, hints at its function and its origin, and this material form contains divine grace by virtue of its holy origin. Peter Lombard (circa 1152) writes that a sacrament is "a sign of the grace of God and a form of invisible grace, so that it bears its image and exists as its cause."[5]

One of the most comprehensive and useful contemporary guides we can use to illuminate the sacramental theology of the medieval church (and to identify some of the central issues for medieval theologians concerning the practical carrying-out of the sacraments) is the *Summa Theologiae* of St. Thomas Aquinas (d. 1274, writing c. 1271), a substantial three-volume work divided clearly according to questions which Aquinas proposes and subsequently answers. The beginning of the third volume of the *Summa* is a long treatment of the sacraments and their operation. Aquinas takes great pains to explain what a sacrament does and how it works, both outwardly and inwardly.

Aquinas is also very clear that sacraments are necessary for the salvation of Christian people, primarily because human nature tends toward engagement with material things, both in ordinary activity and in sinning, and also because of material happenings

[3] "Decree for the Armenians," in James F. White, *Documents of Christian Worship* (Louisville, KY: Westminster John Knox, 1992), 128.

[4] *On the Sacraments of the Christian Faith* I.9, trans. Roy J. Deferarri in *Hugh of Saint Victor on the Sacraments of the Christian Faith* (Cambridge, MA: Medieval Academy of America, 1951), 155.

[5] Peter Lombard, "Distinction I.2–7," trans. Owen R. Ott, in *The Four Books of Sentences* IV, *Library of Christian Classics* 10 (London: SCM Press, 1956), 338–41.

that one may be led to the spiritual.[6] The seven sacraments, of which the Eucharist is the most central (it contains materially the body of Christ), are an instrumental cause of grace, which at a more basic level come from Christ's passion.[7]

It seems to have been a priority for Aquinas, probably echoing contemporary concerns, to outline in which circumstances, and with what formulations, a sacrament should be celebrated, and whether less-than-ideal circumstances would invalidate the efficacy of the sacrament. In every case, writes Aquinas, words and actions suggest themselves by virtue of similarity to the sacramental action, but he finds it necessary to explain, for example, the use of water in baptism as a representation of spiritual cleansing. Aquinas holds that specific forms and specific words should be used (quoting Augustine, "What else is a corporeal sacrament but a kind of visible word?"), although he allows that if a minister inadvertently misspeaks, the sacrament remains valid as long as the essential sense of the statement is not disrupted.[8] The reason for this is that ministers, being human, function as "instruments" for the principal agent (God), so it is possible that even heretics, schismatics, and unbelievers can confer true sacraments, "provided that the other essentials be true,"[9] although it is not advisable that the faithful should receive from them.[10] Nevertheless, it is important that true intention, in normal circumstances, is present, because intentionality defines the meaning of the words and symbols by which the sacrament is celebrated.[11] On the subject of the words of consecration in the Eucharist, Aquinas holds that the words and expressions of Christ as enacted by the minister are the key element: "Since these words are uttered in the person of Christ [by the minister], it is from His command that they receive their instru-

[6] Thomas Aquinas, *Summa Theologiae* (ST) III, q. 61, a. 1.

[7] ST III, q. 62.

[8] Ibid., q. 60.

[9] Ibid., q. 64, a. 1, 5, 8, 9.

[10] Ibid., q. 82, a. 8.

[11] Ibid., q. 64, a. 8.

mental power."[12] The transformation of the bread and wine into Christ's body and blood through consecration is clearly outlined as well: Aquinas shows that the accidents (the material, tangible forms) of the bread and wine remain after the consecration, but that their substance is that of Christ's body and blood: "hence this is not a formal, but a substantial conversion; nor is it a kind of natural movement: but, with a name of its own, it can be called transubstantiation."[13] This doctrine of transubstantiation had been expressed very clearly in the doctrines of the Fourth Lateran Council (1215) which established that "Jesus . . . is both priest and sacrifice, whose body and blood are truly contained in the sacrament of the altar under the species of bread and wine by the transubstantiation of bread into body and wine into blood through divine power: that through the perfecting of the mystery of unity we receive of him from himself, that which he received from us."[14] Since the sacrifice of Christ, which is enacted through the person of the priest each time the Eucharist is celebrated, has already taken place, Aquinas shows that "the thing signified [i.e., the replacement of the substance of the bread and wine by the substance of the body and blood] must be present instantaneously."[15] In this matter, but also in all others which he treats, Aquinas gives forms of words and coherent explanations for matters which are difficult to define or discuss, and thereby places most other sources of insight about the liturgy, and the lay experience of worship, in his debt. The doctrine of transubstantiation strongly affected the way the faithful interacted with the sacrament of the Eucharist; in fact, an awareness of transubstantiation was the main influence on lay and clerical experience of, and participation in, the sacrament.

Despite the high esteem accorded the consecrated elements, the faithful did not normally receive the bread and wine themselves. Rather, it was customary for the priest to consume the bread and wine, and confer the grace of the sacrament to the rest of the clerics

[12] Ibid., q. 78, a. 4.
[13] Ibid., q. 75, a. 4.
[14] Printed in White, *Documents*, 194.
[15] ST III, q. 78, a. 5.

through the kissing of a pax-board, a special decorative implement for conveying the Peace, which the congregation was also encouraged to venerate.

Transubstantiation was also a cause for special veneration of the consecrated elements, which in addition to being displayed in the course of the Eucharist itself were usually reserved within the body of the church in a pyx or tabernacle. In addition to devotions carried out inside the church, there were some occasions when the consecrated bread was carried in procession outside the building and into the community. The late medieval procession on Palm Sunday often began with the sacrament outside the walls of the church (or sometimes outside the walls of the town), after which it made its way along the processional route into the church, representing in a very literal way the entry of Christ (understood to be really present in the consecrated Host), supported by crowds with palms, into Jerusalem, the place of his sacrifice and resurrection, represented by the church in which that sacrifice and manifestation of his body and blood were enacted daily in the Eucharist. Similarly, the consecrated elements played a predictably central role in the feast of Corpus Christi (the body of Christ), which was a celebration expressly of the institution of the Eucharist and a particular opportunity to venerate the sacrament.

LITURGY IN LIFE

It is quite clear that there were many opportunities for the faithful to be present, though not for them to become engaged with the action, at the Eucharist, but there is less evidence, and there would have been conceivably less motivation, for their attendance at other services (for instance the daily Office) without such a dramatic spiritual function, enacted in a language other than their own, and in which they could not otherwise participate, in a place in the church (the quire) into which they could not see. At the Mass, it was possible to follow some of the action by listening for the bell which accompanied the start of the Canon of the Mass and the consecration, but most of the time lay people must have been engaged in private prayer (unless otherwise occupied). Increasingly in this period these devotions may have taken the form of prayers expressly provided for the laity when hearing Mass which might be memorized or, in the case of the literate, found in books of Hours or Primers, volumes which also supplied the reader with the texts of popular Offices, especially the votive Office of the Blessed Virgin Mary and the Office of the Dead, as well as popular prayers and devotional exercises, a liturgical calendar, psalms, and other spiritual resources. For the less literate, these books, especially the more elaborate and expensive ones, also contained pictures onto which the faithful could fix an adoring gaze, or which helped to convey the message of the text.

Further resources for pious reflection would have been found in the art and architecture of the church, much of it visible to the congregation. Here stories from Scripture depicting the life, death, and resurrection of Christ were often painted on the walls for the edification of illiterate Christians who did not have the benefit of reading the Bible for themselves, alongside representations of Jesus, Mary, and the saints, all with their identifying attributes (i.e., the keys of St. Peter) which usually identified the reason for their sainthood.[16] Some such wall-paintings survive today in medieval churches, and it is clear that some of their features, especially the grotesque and visceral images, would have remained in the memories of viewers. Central in function as well as placement was the often substantial crucifix on the rood-screen, which occupied the vision of the faithful in the nave.

In addition to all these works of art, the faithful knew they were in a building where the sacrament was reserved and where, consequently, Christ was substantially present, and where saints' relics, literal embodiments of holy persons, were often deposited. Such objects, like the sacrament, required veneration, as if the saints themselves were physically present. Statues, images, side-altars, and chapels outside the choir were sometimes the destination of processions which would venerate these physical manifestations or locations of sanctity, or offer prayers. Seeing one of these processions would intensify the devotional significance of these objects

[16] A practice referred to by John Ruskin in, among other essays, *The Bible of Amiens*.

normally to be found in the lay worshippers' own space. By contrast, images, crosses, and relics, as well as the pyx containing the sacrament, were covered by veils in Lent, encouraging an atmosphere of austerity in the penitential season. By contrast, during the observance of Holy Week and Easter, as well as on great feast days, the processions and additional ceremonies heightened the experience of worship and undoubtedly stimulated devotion to saints as well as particular Christological and Marian observances. Among these observances, the Transfiguration, the Holy Name of Christ, and the Visitation of the Blessed Virgin Mary saw new liturgical attention in the later Middle Ages. The bodily or personified nature of many of these new occasions is worth consideration, particularly in light of the bodily nature of representations of the suffering Christ (as opposed to such images being focused on the resurrection).

In a different sensory vein, the sounds audible in the nave during worship could be clearly distinguished: in practice, spoken text does not carry well, even in a small space, compared with intoned words (sung to a single note), which are clearer. While the precise words of items set to music would be perhaps less identifiable, the melodies themselves, where they appeared as part of the daily round of worship, would have been memorable.

Sometimes in larger institutions listeners would hear the stirring sound of improvised polyphony. The sonic experience of worship would, for frequent attendees, itself help to pass the time and to keep track of the action in the sanctuary, not just when the bell rang. Such a sonic experience would not have been foreign to anchorites, people withdrawn from the world not in monastic life or in hermitage, but shut away by their own desire in cells from which they would rarely if ever emerge. Often in the Middle Ages, anchorites were attached to churches where they would be able to hear and perhaps see the liturgy going on, and at other times devote themselves entirely to prayer and devotion. The most familiar such person is surely Julian of Norwich, known best as a spiritual writer (d. ca 1416), author of the *Revelations of Divine Love*, a moving book of mystical experiences. The liturgical experience of lay people outside the choir may have been no more extensive, despite their freedom, than that of anchorites.

It should now be clear that the faithful who attended liturgical services were more or less left alone, except during interventions of clerics into the nave, for instance when they delivered readings from atop the rood-screen, or when a procession exited the choir in order to make a circuit around the nave. This is not at all to say that they were ignored—indeed the services were offered on behalf of the faithful, and they were prayed for according to their various circumstances. Nor should it be assumed that their participation was in some way not elicited or expected (despite the fact that it was avowedly not "active" in the twentieth-century definition). In addition to their prayers joining those of the clergy and choir and those of all Christians throughout the world in mutual thanksgiving and appeal for intercession, the attention of the faithful at worship was captured by private devotion, either wordlessly or in familiar textual forms. The interiorization of piety, inspired by an impulse toward penance for sins committed, both one's own and the sins of humankind, was the same instinct that inspired the endowment of chantries for the benefit of the departed; a most appropriate act of charity in an age where death was rarely far from daily life and which, at certain times, was inflicted with terror by visitations of plague and war. The medieval spiritual preoccupation with death will be explored in the following section, which provides a translation of part of the Office of the Dead, together with an explanation of the function of this very popular liturgical observance which encapsulates a number of the broader themes of medieval worship: penance, salvation, and bodily experience.

"DELIVER ME, O LORD": THE OFFICE OF THE DEAD

Unlike many liturgical rites, the Office of the Dead appeared in various guises: as a daily votive observance, both as part of an expanded pattern of the Office observed in some communities and in endowed chantries; as part of the obsequies for the deceased; and, as laid out here, as the proper Office for All Souls' Day. It owed its importance in part to widespread devotional awareness in books of Hours available to the literate laity as well as in psalters and other fuller liturgical books, and its influence was such that some of the non-Scriptural texts (and indeed at least one melody, *Dies irae*, shared with the proper Mass for the Dead) are still part of our cultural consciousness. The English words "placebo" and "dirge" have their origins in *Placebo* and *Dirige*, the opening words of Vespers and Matins of the Dead respectively, although the texts of the Office of the Dead themselves have gone out of currency.

Although it has close seasonal associations with All Souls' Day (November 2), the Office of the Dead had its origins as a separate, votive commemoration before the institution of the *Commendatio animarum* (commendation of souls) in the eleventh century.[17] The English Catholic antiquary Edmund Bishop argued that the Office as a devotion could be attested before 817 as a practice encouraged by the monastic reformer Benedict of Aniane, though more recently the liturgist Knud Ottosen distrusts any Roman origin for the Office before the ninth century.[18] It is a matter of debate whether the Office began as a regularly scheduled monastic observance to pray for the departed souls of a community, as has sometimes been proposed, or whether it was used in place of the daily Office for the vigil of a funeral, the usage which seems to have been the most frequent in the later Middle Ages. There are compelling arguments on both sides: in support of the vigil of a funeral, it ought to be noted that the liturgy has special prayers used in the presence of the corpse; on the contrary, the foundation in the later Middle Ages of chantry chapels which were enjoined *in their statutes* to say the Office of the Dead for specified individuals may hint at origins of the Office in a votive, perpetual observance. Obvious is the relation of the Office to the doctrine of Purgatory and the belief that succor of the souls therein could be obtained by the prayers of the faithful. Purgatory as a distinct place between Paradise and Hell did not become an authoritative doctrine before 1170,[19] but there are numerous Scriptural and patristic references to forgiveness in the world to come (e.g., Matt 12:31-32) and purgation through fire. The Office of the Dead, with its readings inevitably from Job who

[17] Ottosen, *The Responsories and Versicles of the Latin Office of the Dead* (Aarhus: Aarhus University Press, 1993), 42.

[18] Ottosen, *Responsories and Versicles*, 35; quoting Edmund Bishop.

[19] Ottosen, *Responsories and Versicles*, 47 ; and see Jacques Le Goff, *La Naissance du Purgatoire* (Paris: Gallimard, 1981), 177–80.

complains of his torments and waits for deliverance, can be easily interpreted in the light of Purgatory: Job's grievances become those of the souls in the afterlife awaiting deliverance from Christ.[20] Its pervasiveness in manuscript and printed sources can perhaps also explain its importance to contemporary literature (the influence of liturgies for the dead on the writers Dante and Petrarch, for example[21]) and the intellectual exploration of death and the afterlife: as Ottosen put it, the Office of the Dead is a human response to the "eternal questions . . . whence do I come, where shall I go?" that "make . . . each human being a theologian."[22] The Office was an expression of, and an interaction with, what has been described by Jacques Le Goff as the essential medieval theological concept—Purgatory—and by its consistency and frequency of appearance in liturgical books, in its enormously frequent observance in public and private, and its lasting cultural resonances, we are assured of an unusually accurate portrait of medieval thinking on the subject.[23]

By the later Middle Ages, the Office of the Dead was an extremely widely disseminated observance, appearing in service books sometimes as a separate section (for votive use) and frequently in the Sanctorale for All Souls' Day. Books of Hours and Primers, as well as other personal books, often contained the Office of the Dead with the Offices of the Blessed Virgin Mary and the Cross. The sungtexts for the Dead (that is, the proper texts that were sung in contrast to lessons and rubrics) existed in unvarying patterns in a variety of local and regional liturgical uses, including the Use of York, which was normative in northern England in the late Middle Ages and whose form is reproduced in the version below. This is not to suggest any preeminence on the part of the

[20] Ottosen, *Responsories and Versicles*, 47.

[21] See Ronald L. Martinez, "Dante's Forese, the Book of Job, and the Office of the Dead: A Note on *Purgatorio* 23," *Dante Studies*, 120 (2002): 1–16; and "Mourning Laura in the *Canzoniere*: Lessons from Lamentations," *Modern Language Notes*, 118 (2003): 1–45.

[22] Ottosen, *Responsories and Versicles*, 385.

[23] Jacques Le Goff, *La Naissance du Purgatoire* (Paris: Gallimard, 1981); or, trans. Arthur Goldhammer (London: Scolar Press, 1984).

York Use in question, merely to choose one of the many possible, authorized versions which were used across Western Europe. The responsories have clear Scriptural references; and the overall structure of the Office does not vary. The point here is that Vespers, Matins, and Lauds of the Dead, or some portion thereof, had become a daily observance even in secular communities around the twelfth century, as well as in religious houses, commemorations, and chantries. Its apparent fixity may be a result of its ubiquity in an ecclesiastical context, fostering the memorization of its texts and melodies through frequent repetition, no doubt helped by the proliferation of manuscript copies.

THE TEXT OF THE OFFICE OF THE DEAD

This version of Matins of the Dead is transcribed from the first printed Breviary according to the Use of York (the dominant liturgical tradition in the north of England), which was printed in 1493 by Johannes Hamman in Venice. Psalms (as in the original) are not reproduced in full, nor are the readings from the Book of Job, for which complete references are given. The dialogues that open, close, and signpost the service are not included for the sake of simplicity.

As has been stated, Matins is the longest of the components of the Office, the most distinctive, and the most complex in structure. Here, it is divided into three *nocturns*, each with three antiphons and psalms preceding three lessons from Scripture, responsories, and verses. Sequential reading will help to identify some of the themes which are carried between antiphons and psalms (which were complementary) and lessons and responsories (which enjoyed a similar relationship). Translations of Biblical passages are drawn from the Authorized Version, and where possible the other texts follow familiar textual formulations.

IN DIE OMNIUM ANIMARUM AD MATUTINAS	**ALL SOULS' DAY MATINS**
FIRST NOCTURN	
A. Dirige Domine meus, in conspectu tuo viam meam. Ps 5. Verba mea auribus.	A. Make my way straight before thy face, O Lord my God. Ps 5. Consider my words, O Lord.

A. Converte, Domine, et eripe animam meam: quoniam non est in morte qui memor sit tui. Ps 6. Domine ne in furore.	A. Turn thee, O Lord, and deliver my soul: for in death no man remembereth thee. Ps 6. O Lord, rebuke me not.
A. Nequando rapiat ut leo animam meam, dum non est qui redimat, neque qui salvum faciat. Ps 7. Domine Deus meus, in te speravi: salvum me fac ex omnibus persequentibus me, et líbera me.	A. Lest he tear my soul like a lion, while there is none to deliver, or to save. Ps 7. O Lord my God, in thee have I put my trust: save me from all them that persecute me, and deliver me.
Lesson 1 (Job 7:16-21) Parce mihi domine: nihil enim sunt dies mei. Quid est homo quia magnificas eum? Aut quid apponis erga eum cor tuum . . .	Spare me, O Lord, for my days are as a breath. What is man, that thou shouldest magnify him? and that thou shouldest set thine heart upon him . . .
R. Credo quod Redemptor meus vivit, et in novissimo die de terra surrecturus sum, et in carne mea videbo Deum Salvatorem meum. V. Quem visurus sum ego ipse, et non alius, et oculi mei conspecturi sunt. R. Et in carne mea videbo Deum Salvator.	R. I know that my Redeemer liveth, and that he shall stand in the latter day upon the earth, and in my flesh shall I see God my Saviour. V. Whom I shall see for myself, and mine eyes shall behold, and not as a stranger. R. And in my flesh shall I see God my Saviour.
Lesson 2 (Job 10:1-7) Tedet animam meam vite mee, dimittam adversum me eloquium meum, loquar in amaritudine anime mee . . .	My soul is weary of my life: I will give free course to my complaint; I will speak in the bitterness of my soul . . .
R. Qui Lazarum resuscitasti a monumento foetidum, Tu eis, Domine, dona requiem, et locum indulgentiae. V. Qui venturus es judicare vivos et mortuos, et saeculum per ignem. R. Tu eis, Domine, dona requiem, et locum indulgentiae.	R. Thou that didst raise Lazarus from the grave after that he had begun to corrupt, Do thou, O Lord, grant them rest and a place of forgiveness. V. Thou who shalt come to judge the quick and the dead, and the world by fire. R. Do thou, O Lord, grant them rest and a place of forgiveness.
Lesson 3 (Job 10:8-12) Manus tue fecerunt me, et plasmaverunt me totum in circuitu: et sic repente precípitas me . . .	Thine hands have made me and fashioned me together round about; and yet wouldest thou so suddenly destroy me . . .

R. Domine, quando veneris iudicare terram, ubi me abscondam a vultu ire tue? Quia peccavi nimis in vita mea. V. Commissa mea pavesco, et ante te erubesco: dum veneris iudicare, noli me condemnare. R. Quia peccavi nimis in vita mea.	R. O Lord, when thou comest to judge the earth, whither shall I hide me from the presence of thy wrath? For I have sinned grievously in my life. V. I begin to fear my misdeeds, and blush before thee: when thou comest to judgment, condemn me not. R. For I have sinned grievously in my life.
SECOND NOCTURN	
A. In loco pascue ibi me collocavit. Ps 23. Dominus regit me.	A. In a place of the pasture shall he feed me. Ps 23. The Lord is my shepherd.
A. Delicta iuventutis mee et ignorancias meas ne memineris, Domine. Ps 25. Ad te Domine levavi animam meam.	A. O remember not the sins and offences of my youth, Lord. Ps 25. Unto thee, O Lord, will I lift up my soul.
A. Credo videre bona Domini in terra viventium. Ps 27. Dominus illuminatio mea.	A. I believe verily to see the goodness of the Lord in the land of the living. Ps 27. The Lord is my light.
Lesson 4 (Job 13:23-28) Responde mihi: Quantas habeo iniquitates, et peccata, scelera mea, atque delicta ostende mihi.	Answer thou me: How many are mine iniquities and misdeeds? Make me to know my transgressions and offences.
R. Heu mihi, Domine, quia peccavi nimis in vita mea. Quid faciam miser? Ubi fugiam, nisi ad te, Deus meus. Miserere mei, dum veneris in novissimo die. V. Anima mea turbata est valde: sed tu, Domine, succure ei. R. Dum veneris in novissimo die.	R. Woe is me, O Lord, for I have grievously sinned in my life! What shall I do, wretched man that I am? Whither shall I flee, but unto thee, my God? Have mercy upon me, when thou comest at the last day. V. My soul is sore troubled; but, Lord, be thou my helper. R. When thou comest at the last day.
Lesson 5 (Job 14:1-6) Homo natus de muliere, brevi vivens tempore, repletur multis miseriis. Qui quasi flos egreditur, et conteritur, et fugit velud umbra, et nunquam in eodem statu permanet . . .	Man that is born of a woman hath but a short time to live, and is full of misery. He cometh forth like a flower, and is cut down; he fleeth as it were a shadow, and never continueth in one stay . . .

R. Ne recorderis peccata mea, Domine, dum veneris iudicare seculum per ignem. V. Dirige, Domine, Deus meus, in conspectu tuo viam meam. R. Dum veneris iudicare seculum per ignem.	R. Remember not my sins, O Lord, when thou shalt come to judge the world by fire. V. Make thy way plain, O Lord my God, before my face. R. When thou shalt come to judge the world by fire.
Lesson 6 (Job 14:13-16) Quis mihi hoc tribuat, ut in inferno protegas me, et abscondas me, donec pertranseat furor tuus, et constituas mihi tempus, in quo recorderis mei . . .	O that thou wouldest hide me in the grave; that thou wouldest keep me secret, until thy wrath be past; that thou wouldest appoint me a set time, and remember me . . .
R. Libera me, Domine, de viis inferni. Qui portas aereas confregisti, et visitasti infernum, et dedisti eis lumen ut viderent te qui erant in paenis tenebrarum. V. Clamantes et dicentes, advenisti redemptor noster. R. Qui portas aereas confregisti, et visitasti infernum, et dedisti eis lumen ut viderent te qui erant in paenis tenebrarum.	R. Deliver me, O Lord, from the paths of hell, even thou that didst break the gates of brass; even thou that didst visit hell, and gavest light to the inhabitants thereof, that they might see thee who were in the pains of darkness. V. Them that were crying aloud and saying, Thou hast come, O our redeemer. R. Even thou that didst break the gates of brass; even thou that didst visit hell, and gavest light to the inhabitants thereof, that they might see thee who were in the pains of darkness.
THIRD NOCTURN	
A. Complaceat tibi, Domine, ut eripias me: Domine, ad adiuvandum me respice. Ps 40. Exspectans expectavi Dominum.	A. Let it be thy pleasure to deliver me, O Lord: make haste, O Lord, to help me. Ps 40. I waited patiently for the Lord.
A. Sana, Domine, animam meam, quia peccavi tibi. Ps 41. Beatus qui intelligit	A. Heal my soul, O Lord, for I have sinned against thee. Ps 41. Blessed is he that considereth.
A. Sitivit anima mea ad Deum vivum: quando veniam, et apparebo ante faciem Domini? Ps 42. Quemadmodum desiderat cervus	A. My soul is athirst for God, yea even for the living God: when shall I come to appear before the presence of God? Ps 42. Like as the hart desireth.
Lesson 7 (Job 17:1-4, 11-15) Spiritus meus attenuabitur, dies mei breviabuntur, et solum mihi superest sepulcrum . . .	My breath will wax feebler, and my days fewer, and there is nothing before me but the grave . . .

R. Peccantem me quotídie, et non me pœnitentem, timor mortis conturbat me: Quia in inferno nulla est redemptio, miserere mei, Deus, et salva me. V. Deus, in nomine tuo salvum me fac, et in virtute tua líbera me. R. Quia in inferno nulla est redemptio, miserere mei, Deus, et salva me.	R. It is upon such an one as myself, who doth sin often and repent seldom, that the fear of death befalleth. Because in hell there is no redemption, have mercy upon me O God, and save me. V. Save me, O God, for thy Name's sake, and deliver me in thy strength. R. Because in hell there is no redemption, have mercy upon me O God, and save me.
Lesson 8 (Job 19:20-27) Pelli mee, consumptis carnibus, adhesit os meum, et derelicta sunt tantummodo labia circa dentes meos.	 My flesh is consumed, my bone cleaveth unto my skin, and there remaineth not round my teeth save the skin of my lips.
R. Deus eterne, in cuius humana conditio potestate consistit, animas omnium fidelium defunctorum, quesumus, ab omnibus absolve peccatis. Ut penitentie fructum quem voluntas eorum optavit, preventi morte. V. Qui in cruce positus latronem sero penitentem suscepisti, eorum precamur pie peccata dele. R. Ut penitentie fructum quem voluntas eorum optavit, preventi morte non perdant.	R. Eternal God, we beseech thee that by the power of thy human condition thou might absolve the souls of the faithful departed of all their sins, that by penitence, they might not lose the reward that their will desired. V. Who, set on a cross, received the penitent thief, we pray thee tenderly, erase their sins. R. That by penitence, they might not lose the reward that their will desired.
Lesson 9 (Job 10:18-22) Quare de vulva eduxisti me? qui utinam consumptus essem, ne oculus me videret.	 Wherefore then hast thou brought me forth out of the womb? O that I had given up the ghost, and no eye had seen me!
R. Libera me, Domine, de morte eterna in die illa tremenda. Quando caeli movendi sunt et terra, dum veneris judicare seculum per ignem. V. Dies illa, dies irae, calamitatis et miserie, dies magna et amara valde. R. Quando caeli movendi sunt et terra, dum veneris judicare seculum per ignem.	R. Deliver me, O Lord, from everlasting death in that fearful day. When the heavens and the earth shall be shaken: when thou shalt come to judge the world by fire. V. Woe is me, for the day of wrath, calamity, and misery, the great day of exceeding bitterness. R. When the heavens and the earth shall be shaken: when thou shalt come to judge the world by fire.
V. Audivi vocem de celo dicentem: R. Beati mortui qui in Domino moriuntur.	V. I heard a voice from heaven saying: R. Blessed are the dead who die in the Lord.

Readers will be able to guess some of the effects of the perpetual, daily recitation or hearing of this Office: the repetition of the texts, rich in imagery and in some of the most hopeless dialogues in Scripture, cannot but inspire an internalization of their sentiments, which will stand as the foundation of belief. It is no surprise, given that literary elements of this medieval Office remain in present-day parlance, that liturgy here, as in so many other cases, offers simultaneously a source and representation of medieval theological understanding, and an inspired source of literary reflection on death: it is an intellectual locus where memory is employed, and where memories are made.

MEDIEVAL WORSHIP AND MEMORY

Memory is an undervalued facet of participation in the medieval liturgy, partly because both we and medieval worshippers insist that despite the frequency of celebration of some rites, the complexity of their order (as seen above) necessitates special books which govern precisely their performance and serve as a ready reference. Books of the liturgy are literally fragments of past times, helping us to engage with a complex network of artistic and intellectual outputs. They account for a significant proportion of the written witness to the Middle Ages, an almost unsurpassed repository of intellectual outputs. They are also the written record of a central facet of medieval life—the daily round of worship—which inspired and informed a great deal of contemporary thought, devotion, and scholarly work. Quite sensibly and predictably, we imagine the book as a score, containing in precise and accurate detail the totality of what was required for the task of performing directly and precisely from the book.

Yet this must be a rather one-sided interpretation of the performance of the medieval liturgy. An understanding of medieval reading will benefit from considering the concepts of *lectio*, as in *lectio divina*, in which the derivation of meaning from text is but one aspect of the process, and *ruminatio*, a process by which the text is digested, read and reread, and regurgitated and read again, rather than browsed, skimmed, or sight-read, with the objective not only of recollection but also of thinking around the text in question. Reading is bound up with composition and comprehension as well as performance. We would be remiss if we failed to suggest how this applied to the performance of liturgical text and music, for which repetition and internalization are a commonplace. All of this activity took place within an intertextual matrix linking present and past experience, and knowledge of a corpus of text and music, whose interconnections and insights are not capable of being perceived or fully understood by anyone who might be satisfied by an invariable, authoritative text that dismisses textual variation as error rather than as evidence.

Like the lay people in the nave who had to interpret what they could see and hear of the hidden worship in the choir, clerics had to interlace their experience of performing the liturgy with their own previous experiences and memories of worship, their personal faith however constituted, and the stimuli presented in the nave. In this nexus of memory, experience, and action, the interpreted contents of all available liturgical books (available either physically or in the memories of their readers), as well as the collective memory of the worshipping community and the particular circumstances of the event, all constitute the definitive form of the rite, its performance. It is this plurality of sources and influences, all with unpredictable interrelationships, that ensured that there was *never* a universal, uniform, authoritative written version of the liturgy in the late Middle Ages, a fact which must be carefully considered before embracing the idea of producing what purports to be one.[24] (This state of affairs stands in contrast to what we have encountered in previous chapters, where liturgy is much more consistent and controlled, but such a level of fixity must be seen as a relatively recent development that was possible and desirable from the nineteenth century onward.) In every place of worship the influences on what was to happen were different, because different people with different memories and experiences were responsible for moving from remembered act to act rendered present. The written witness *reflects* imperfectly the performed act (which in its own brief moment of existence is always complete and correct, so long as it

[24] Conceivably, this will probably also have been true of the various manuscript service books in a single medieval cathedral.

satisfies Aquinas's notion of correct intention) which no written witness can duplicate. In considering the medieval liturgy, then, we are inexorably drawn to the material and written evidence, but also need to remember that worship, and its undertaking, were always shaped and influenced by those persons who performed and witnessed it. As Mary Carruthers has written, anamnesis (the recalling of the past) and by extension the anamnesis of reading, listening, performing, and recalling, is not the reproduction of a discrete thing but "a personal event, with full phenomenological status."[25] Liturgy always communicates cultural value and illustrates some of the context in which it exists. Medieval worship existed to illustrate and to revere divine beauty and, as such, was much more than mere decoration or superficial piety. For medieval men and women, the material expression of worship was the simplest and most natural method of perceiving the divine and bringing it into the world.

[25] Mary Carruthers, *The Book of Memory: A Study of Memory in Medieval Culture* (Cambridge, UK: Cambridge University Press, 2008), 77.

CHAPTER 5

"A School for the Lord's Service"

Indeed, nothing is to be preferred to the work of God.
—St. Benedict

The new status of Christianity as a legal religion from AD 313 onward, as a result of the acceptance of the faith by the Roman Emperor Constantine, was of central importance to its further development and expansion, neither of which could have been imagined unless the Christian community became a part of the fabric of wider society. More specifically, legalization had a very great influence on the ways in which the church carried out its public worship and how such public acts were understood by both their performers and by a wider, more diverse, and much expanded Christian people, not all of whom had been tested in their faith by persecution.

Before the "Peace of Constantine," as the legitimization of Christianity was known, the church was obliged to celebrate its rites and carry out its public prayer in secret. Clandestine gatherings of Christians had, in words and actions, recollected and enlivened the memorial of Christ's body and blood through the sharing of bread and wine in concealed, disguised house-churches. They had prayed in these places in secret, and it was in these gatherings, and only there, that Christians could meet one another in the mutual recognition of their faith. In the generations that followed the conversion of the Emperor, it was not only legal, but quasi-obligatory, for all to become Christians. Church buildings, designed in the spacious but simple basilica style which had been used for public buildings of the Roman Empire, began to join other important institutional edifices in settlements. In these buildings—proof of the newly permanent, settled character of the church—were the beginnings of overt, recognized communities of faith, now part of the establishment, and the start of the regularly organized schedule of prayer that in later centuries came to be the defining element and the most important work of religious institutions. Nonclandestine prayer, at which the faithful could be present (but from which, increasingly, they remained separate), began to take a form which was determined, at least in part, by the characteristics, cultural practices, and level of competence of the performers. This was also the time of the earliest religious communities of coenobites, who lived in a community founded as a natural outgrowth of the practices of self-denying hermits who disciplined their minds and bodies in the desert, tempted like Christ.

It is worth pointing out that it had now become possible to live as a Christian outside the confines of undercover worship. Because an increasingly large proportion of the population was Christian, not all believers in a locality might be at the same service, and it became ordinary to pray for family or members of the local community who were not personally present. As the monastic houses grew and their skills at collective worship improved, liturgical forms, especially for the Divine Office, were expanded and precisely organized. The burden of contribution to the form of the liturgy itself began to lie more with the specialists who were performing it than with the others who were present. As the number of clergy grew, so did their responsibilities for a wider community, not all of whom were communicants. The Mass took on a more private atmosphere, moving from community celebration at which persecuted local Christians were present despite the risks, to a more efficient rite, sometimes attended by the celebrant alone, making the sacrifice of the Mass on behalf of all the faithful.

This chapter helps to establish some of the framework for the theology of subsequent centuries which we have already examined. Two councils helped to establish the teachings of the Church which, with its new legal status, was now capable of organizing itself transregionally. The Council of Nicaea (AD 325) was the source of one of universal Christianity's central statements of faith, the

Nicene Creed. The Council of Chalcedon (AD 451), in addition to affirming the equality of the two cities of Rome and Constantinople, pronounced final judgment on the equality of Christ's divine and human natures, emphasizing that he was truly God and truly man. The *Rule* of St. Benedict of Nursia (d. 550) is the inspiration for the founding and florescence of Western monasticism, reformed and reshaped by the Cluniac reforms of the tenth century as well as the reforms of Pope Gregory VII.

Most notably, though, liturgy became an important part of the political and ecclesiastical program of Charlemagne, the first Holy Roman Emperor. Charlemagne's personal efforts to promulgate the Roman Liturgy, complete with those practices particular to the pope's own celebrations, throughout the Frankish realms, make for exciting and captivating reading. They demonstrate the degree to which worship and its forms were associated with and played a role in temporal and spiritual politics, illustrated by the informed care and concern exercised by the emperor over the liturgies celebrated by his own retinue, as well as in his wider realms.

WHY WORSHIP?

For the first time, the practice of the Christian religion, including as a central feature the gathering of the faithful in public, purpose-built churches, was legal and increasingly obligatory. Acts of worship, then, were the *de facto* meeting place for communities and their principal means of consolidation. As an official state religion, Christianity also appropriated and repurposed a multitude of pagan practices from the many small-scale cults which preceded it. For those who sought to discover or impose influence, Charlemagne among them, this community-building function of liturgy served not only to strengthen congregations in a spiritual sense, but also to underline the foundation of an empire both holy and Roman, and the erudition of its ruler in spiritual matters. In the new monastic communities, public worship ordered and filled the day. It provided monks and nuns with a rich vocabulary for prayer, devotion, and study. For ordinary people, too, attending church was a focal point for personal devotion and, while not an overt opportunity to become involved with the liturgical action, participation by being present at public acts of worship was nevertheless a crucial element of spirituality, as well as an indicator of the spiritual and cultural value of the rites.

WHAT HAPPENED?

Following the Peace of Constantine, it was possible to worship in groups in public without fear of persecution, and consequently the liturgy was able to make use of greatly expanded spaces for worship, including public spaces, both to accommodate larger congregations and as an exercise in civic pageantry. In subsequent centuries, distinctive cultures and identities surrounding the institutions in which Christians met and prayed were free to develop. In communities of professed religious, a "little rule for beginners," set out by St. Benedict, was built on the customs of the earliest gatherings of religious, and began to establish the particulars of the monastic pattern of worship throughout the day and year. Public worship, now carried out by dedicated clergy, took on new ceremonial and formal complexity, and the active role of lay participants within the action was necessarily diminished. Local rites, having developed organically and having taken their uniqueness from the communities' cultural experience and historical, liturgical, and architectural context, were replaced across the Holy Roman Empire with a hybrid Romano-Frankish liturgy promulgated for reasons of political expediency by Charlemagne. This meant that one of the earliest efforts at standardization of the liturgy across a wide geographical area was encouraged by worldly pressure rather than ecclesiastical preference.

For the worshipper, adherence to the official state religion was a matter of course. In the new reality, personal piety and understanding of the liturgy and sacraments took on new forms. Where there had been personal engagement in the bringing of gifts of bread and wine to the celebration of the Eucharist, there was passive participation through devotion. Held in common from earlier periods was the centrality of the eucharistic meal, although it was shared in different ways. New theological discussion of the eucharistic sacrifice changed the way Christians approached the Eucharist, especially with an increasing belief, accompanied by doctrinal change, that the real body and blood of Christ were consumed by communicants, although it was far from clear, and a cause of contention, how this was possible.

THE PATTERN OF WORSHIP

Never before the Peace of Constantine had Christians been able to worship their God in ways that the Jews and the civil religion of the Roman Empire had done, in processions and public spectacles as well as in enclosed spaces designed for the purpose. They must have felt that such public liturgies, celebrated with full permission and with rich and spectacular rites, granted their religion the legitimacy that it had lacked for its first three hundred years. Worship was no longer merely a hidden practice celebrated in homes and safe-houses. It was a powerful form of witness to the Gospel and a bellwether for the internalization of Christian doctrine and practices in society. It was only fitting that God should be worshipped with all solemnity, gravity, and earnestness.

Even before Charlemagne, the liturgy of Rome was very much the goal to which other regions aspired, and by around AD 700, when Roman practices, in all their ceremonial detail, were depicted in a document called *Ordo Romanus Primus*, the worship celebrated by the pope had reached untold heights of ritual and complexity, necessitating the recording of the action (less so the spoken and sung texts that the action accompanied and were recorded elsewhere). Such intricate rites would be unthinkable in a context of hidden, illegal worship. The rites expanded to exploit the increased capacity for grandeur afforded by new spaces for celebration, institutional support in the form of communities of clergy as well as monastic foundations, a greatly expanded number of worshippers, and an imperative for forms of worship to be suitably awe-inspiring. The descriptions of the *Ordines Romani* provide those who did not visit Rome themselves with a vivid description of Roman practices, and they helped to illustrate the ritual, frequently held up as a spectacular and noteworthy specimen, so that it could be copied throughout Western Europe. The *Ordines Romani* give a first glimpse of the rite celebrated throughout the Middle Ages and in more or less unmodified form until the Second Vatican Council (discussed in chapter 1).

Further sources include the Gelasian Sacramentary (circa seventh century), a book of texts for the celebration of the Eucharist that supplies extensive details of the ritual, and the Gregorian Sacramentary, which gives the structures and parts of the eucharistic prayer. The Roman Canon, the one Roman eucharistic prayer witnessed to as early as St. Ambrose in the fourth century, also developed in this period, with few changes to its structure or form until the reforms of Vatican II. There are a limited number of internal options by season or celebration, but the Roman Canon remains a *de facto* expression of liturgical doctrine which, throughout its long history, has developed greatly in the subtleties of its theological understanding. It has, however, remained very much linked to the period addressed by the present chapter by historical and textual precedent.

MONASTICISM AND THE DEVELOPMENT OF COMMUNITY PRAYER

It is almost unthinkable to conceive of the church, historic or present, without the widespread involvement of the religious orders. Yet their foundation lies hundreds of years after the death of Christ, at a time when asceticism and self-denial, which had always been deemed praiseworthy, had been mainly associated with lone hermits living out Christ's temptation in the desert. For reasons of stability and mutual support, ascetics began to join together in communities that eventually allowed for the general foundation and rapid development of clerical community prayer. Such prayer was to become the *raison d'être* of monasteries, which were among the greatest institutions in the West, as well as the highest object of liturgical attention throughout the Middle Ages and beyond.

Accounts of the early history of monasticism frequently begin with the life and example of St. Antony of Egypt, an early Christian who had been inspired by the scriptural account of the Apostles and sought to renounce the world in order to follow Christ's example strictly.[1] In his *Confessions*, St. Augustine wrote that he

[1] Matthew 4:20, cited in Douglas Burton-Christie, *The Word in the Desert: Scripture and the Quest for Holiness in Early Christian Monasticism* (Oxford, UK: University Press, 1993), 214.

among many others had been moved by the story of St. Antony, which was by that time well disseminated within the Christian community.[2]

It is difficult to ignore the effect of Antony and other early hermits when examining the foundation and organization of ascetic ideas. Yet in order to evaluate the popularity of the monastic movement, one must also—and perhaps principally—consider what drew immense numbers of "lay and clerical clientele"[3] to it; numbers that St. Antony himself did not attract. Whereas anchoritic asceticism was practiced by a small but not insignificant number of individuals, the existence of cooperative and enclosed societies demonstrates the popular appeal of the monastic life. The Antonian model of solitude was brought to its "logical conclusion"[4] by the apparent introduction of coenobitic or community monasticism by the monk Pachomius in early fourth-century Egypt.

Peter Brown explains the reverence with which ascetics were treated as reflective of the aspirations of the average Late Roman; their self-control was respected.[5] Scriptural references were sought everywhere as a model for conduct. The example of Jesus' temptation in the desert (cf. Mark 1:12ff) and the exhortation in the Acts of the Apostles (2:44) to renounce possessions were among the texts which reinforced the connection of monasticism to the life of Christ. These were allusions familiar to anchorites as well, but within many of the writings there are biblical references too numerous to mention.[6] It is undoubted that these ascetics committed their lives to the prayerful service of God, sometimes even through acts of

[2] Cited in Burton-Christie, *The Word in the Desert*, 8.

[3] Peter Brown, "The Rise and Function of the Holy Man in Late Antiquity," *The Journal of Roman Studies* 61 (1971): 82.

[4] In Susanna Elm, *Virgins of God: The Making of Asceticism in Late Antiquity* (Oxford: Clarendon, 1996), 283.

[5] Brown, "The Rise and Function of the Holy Man," 81.

[6] Many of these are given in the editions; see especially the *Seventh Letter* of Pachomius in *Pachomian Koinonia: Instructions, Letters, and Other Writings of Saint Pachomius and his Disciples*, ed. and trans. Armand Veilleux, vol. 3. (Kalamazoo, MI: Cistercian Publications, 1982), 69–71; Pachomius cites many edifying passages contained in the New Testament.

extreme self-denial, but maintaining such a lifestyle was understood to be extraordinarily difficult. It was partly out of a wish for stability and support that the first coenobitic communities, groups living a common rule, came to exist.

Some of the first coenobitic religious communities are associated with St. Pachomius, a fourth-century convert turned ascetic, for whom the case for monastic community living was strong. "It is by a favour from God . . . that there appeared upon earth the holy *Koinonia*, by which he made known the life of the apostles to men who desire to follow their model forever."[7] Pachomius had tried the life of the solitary ascetic, living in a hermitage near St. Antony, but a vision instructed him to build a dwelling place for others. This vision, which inspired the construction of a monastery in the abandoned village of Tabennesis, is explained in his First Greek *Life*. This was to be a place where "many people would come . . . to become monks."[8] While the desert remained a popular image in the model of asceticism as typified by Antony, the literature suggests that restrictive urban or community structures were important to its further development. Brown suggests that the conventions of community living had to be transplanted to the desert[9]; similarly, James Goehring even proposes that Pachomius's coenobitic monasticism was the result of "*withdrawal* from the desert"[10] and could be described as a sort of "village asceticism." This establishment of structure can also be seen in the accounts of the institution of the community in the *Lives*, where division of labor and administrative hierarchy were laid out.[11] In contrast to the entirely

[7] "Instructions of Theodore," in *Pachomian Koinonia*, vol. 3, 91.

[8] *The Life of Pachomius: Vita Prima Graeca* 12, trans. Apostolos Athanassakis, Texts and Translations 7, Society of Biblical Literature 2 (Missoula, MT: Scholars Press for the Society of Biblical Literature, 1975), 17.

[9] Brown, "The Rise and Function of the Holy Man," 83.

[10] James E. Goehring, "Withdrawing from the Desert: Pachomius and the Development of Village Monasticism in Upper Egypt," *Harvard Theological Review* 89, no. 3 (July 1996): 270 and 271ff. Emphasis mine.

[11] Cf. the *First Greek Life*, in *The Life of Saint Pachomius and his Disciples. Pachomian Koinonia*, ed. and trans. Armand Veilleux, vol. 1 (Kalamazoo, MI: Cistercian Publications 1980), 315.

isolated dwellings of the Antonian hermits, Pachomius's monasteries were comprised of a series of houses in which the monks lived and celebrated the Office, surrounded by a wall and including a church where they would gather on Saturdays and Sundays for the celebration of Mass.

Pachomius had, of course, tried both eremitic and coenobitic life. In his *Instruction Concerning a Spiteful Monk*, a document which contains many recommendations for virtuous living, Pachomius wrote, "If you cannot get along alone, join another who is living according to the Gospel of Christ, and you will make progress with him. Either listen, or submit to one who listens."[12] A central reason for joining with another was the defense of neophytes against peril. In his *Fourth Letter*, Pachomius wrote:

> Strive with all your strength to follow the custom of the monastery. . . . Thus you will not prepare for [will not condemn yourself to?] the punishment of the age to come . . . nor will you be kept in the bonds of sins, to be condemned . . . [because of] the negligence of the brothers who are with you and co-operate with you, [and who] know that we have transmitted to them very faithfully what we were given by God.[13]

Indeed, the similarity of many coenobitic rules—especially St. Benedict's—to that of Pachomius illustrates how the ideals, precepts, and regulations he promoted were popular enough that they were distributed widely. Whether or not he was the founder (as has been questioned) of coenobitic life, his influence as illustrated in the sources provided "a character that been henceforth unknown"[14] to the movement.

The worship lives of the hermits who lived in the time before communities of religious were very much an individual affair, with some gathering in small groups to say psalms from time to time, and others meeting only on Saturdays and Sundays to worship.

[12] "Instruction Concerning a Spiteful Monk", *Pachomian Koinonia* vol. 3, 19. The account is not dissimilar to his own experience in joining the hermit Palamon.

[13] "Fourth Letter of St Pachomius," *Pachomian Koinonia* vol. 3, 60.

[14] Ibid., 317.

It is worth highlighting that it was at times of worship, in many cases only at these times, that these otherwise isolated men came together. This feature may have contributed to the constancy of the hermits and contributed to the attractiveness of other ways of coming together. A more rigorous pattern of worship necessitated closer gatherings and the building up of communities. Certainly Cassian's *Institutes* help to identify clearly the contemporaneously understood principle that successful communities normally establish a "prescribed system of prayers . . . in their evening assemblies and nocturnal vigils."[15] The use of twelve psalms at services in the evening and at night was believed to be divinely ordained, and the psalms were supplemented with readings from the Old and New Testaments. The repetition of all the psalms in order, sometimes in a very short period of time, helped to put their texts in the mouths and minds of those who participated in the service, and contributed to the shared experience of coming together in community, which could be re-lived in solitude through the words which remained with them.

The *Rule* of St. Benedict, the most famous and successful of all the early monastic rules, was the product of long years of experience on the part of its writer, both as an Antonian-style hermit and as the leader of communities. Benedict's *Rule* dates from about 530, composed probably at Monte Cassino, where his community was established. Benedict probably drew on knowledge of such guides as the rules of St. Basil and St. Pachomius, but also added elements which encouraged the stability, regularity, and communal discipline of a community, among them the subjection in all things to the leaders of the community and the atmosphere of a family group, as well as the avoidance of competition in forms of austerity. In all situations, "all are to follow the teaching of the rule, and no one shall rashly deviate from it. In the monastery no one is to follow his own heart's desire."[16] This obedience to Christ, the *Rule*, and

[15] John Cassian, *Institutes* II 3, 5, 6, in Edgar C.S. Gibson, *Nicene and Post-Nicene Fathers*, 2nd series XI, 205.

[16] The Rule of St. Benedict (hereafter RB) 3.7–8, in *RB 1980: The Rule of St. Benedict in English*, ed. Timothy Fry (Collegeville, MN: Liturgical Press, 1982).

the abbot is frequently mentioned: "The first step of humility is unhesitating obedience, which comes naturally to those who cherish Christ above all."[17] Benedict identifies "tools for good works" including love of God, self-renunciation, and discipline, that he wishes his followers to employ in the "workshop where we are to toil faithfully [namely], the enclosure of the monastery."

He sees prayer and listening to Scripture as essential to the amendment of life: "Listen readily to holy reading, and devote yourself often to prayer. Every day with tears and sighs confess your past sins to God in prayer and change from these evil ways in the future."[18] Among the "twelve steps of humility" prescribed by Benedict is humility in bearing and in heart "at the Work of God [and] in the oratory,"[19] and if mistakes happen to be made, the monk responsible "must make satisfaction there before all. If he does not use this occasion to humble himself, he will be subjected to more severe punishment for failing to correct by humility the wrong committed through negligence. Children, however, are to be whipped for such a fault."[20]

Because the performance of the liturgy was the first and most solemn duty of the community, to fail by making a mistake in the public worship of God was to devalue the work of the whole community. Being complicated in its execution, the liturgy made it easy for one to be humbled in its performance. Benedict also prescribed a penalty to those who came late to services: "he is not to stand in his regular place in choir. He must take the last place of all, or one set apart by the abbot for such offenders, that they may be seen by him and by all, until they do penance by public satisfaction at the end of the Work of God."[21] Penance for serious offences was for the perpetrator to lie prostrate at the feet of the community leaving the oratory, and even when readmitted to the choir, the offender was not to lead psalms or deliver readings until instructed by the abbot.[22]

[17] RB 5.1–2.
[18] RB 4.55–58.
[19] RB 7.62.
[20] RB 45.
[21] RB 43.4–6.
[22] RB Chap. 44.

If a monk committed a "serious fault," he was excluded both from the common table and from the corporate liturgy.[23] It is in this way that the liturgy was for Benedict an instrument of community cohesion and collective participation in the principal work of the monastery: "Brothers," he wrote, "now that we have asked the Lord who will dwell in his tent, we have heard the instruction for dwelling in it, but only if we fulfill the obligations of those who live there."[24]

Correct performance of public worship, arrived at with correct intentions and a good will, was paramount: "We believe that the divine presence is everywhere and that in every place the eyes of the Lord are watching the good and the wicked. But beyond the least doubt we should believe this to be especially true when we celebrate the divine office."[25]

Contained in the rest of Benedict's *Rule* are instructions and advice to ensure that the skill, discipline, and attitude which enable the performance of the liturgy are always present in the community. Some chapters are devoted to specific instructions for the ordering of the day and year according to the patterns of the liturgy, giving particular attention to the Office, the division of the psalms, and the other material which accompanied them. In order to take a position of responsibility in the liturgy, brothers needed the abbot's permission: "No one should presume to read or sing unless he is able to benefit the hearers: let this be done with humility, seriousness and reverence, and at the abbot's bidding."[26] Benedict's prescriptions about activity at various hours of the day are relatively liberal compared to some of the Egyptian ascetics' practices,[27] but he is unstinting about the rigor of the Office: chapter 9 sets out the basic structure of the monastic night office of Matins (also known as Vigils) which became the foundation for the standard monastic pattern throughout Western Europe. The number of services of the Office is laid down: seven times during the day, and once at night:

[23] RB Chap. 25.
[24] RB Prol. 39.
[25] RB 19.1–2.
[26] RB 47.2–4.
[27] RB Chap. 8.

Lauds, Prime, Terce, Sext, None, Vespers, Compline, and Matins. The Little Hours, Vespers, and Compline are laid out clearly but with lesser detail. The psalmody which occupied the greatest proportion of service time is also set down, although Benedict says the precise arrangement is flexible as long as the community says the whole psalter in the course of a week's services: "for monks who in a week's time say less than the full psalter with the customary canticles betray extreme indolence and lack of devotion in their service."[28]

The *Rule* is designed to be edifying, and also to make teaching and learning possible within the daily lives of the community, partly through the teaching of superiors but especially through the liturgy. Benedict allows a choice of readings that give explanations of Scripture from "reputable and orthodox catholic Fathers" as well as from Scripture itself. He also suggests that the order should be amended in summertime when the nights are correspondingly shorter, and even when the community is late to begin the service. Benedict also gives readers a brief summary of the important ways the day's services are influenced by the celebration of a saint's day or by some other occurrence with much attention to practicalities. In all things the *Rule* strives to provide useful, conservative guidance for the actual execution of the duties of the community, seeing worship as the central and most valued element of its work. Because this work is the very reason for which the community exists, it was seen as essential that the monks should "serve the Lord with fear, and again, Sing praise wisely . . . Let us consider, then, how we ought to behave in the presence of God and his angels, and let us stand to sing the psalms in such a way that our minds are in harmony with our voices."[29]

Benedict's *Rule*, described as a "little rule for beginners," seems quite onerous in its demands not only for the rigors of religious life (poverty, chastity, and obedience), but also for good-natured living, stern reproofs for error, and other incongruities which might seem to the modern-day lay reader very difficult to live by. Yet Benedict

[28] RB 18.24.

[29] RB Chap. 19.

clearly identifies his *Rule* as only the beginning of religious perfection, achievable only with the help of the works of the Church Fathers, as well as the Bible, the *Conferences*, the *Institutes*, and the *Lives of the Fathers*, and the *Rule* of St. Basil mentioned by name. "All these are nothing less than tools for the cultivation of virtues; but as for us, they make us blush for shame at being so slothful, so unobservant, so negligent."[30]

In fact, the *Rule* stresses moderation and rational decisions, without any of the extreme conditions of the Desert Fathers which might cause the breakdown of a well-organized monastic community dependent on the good work, fine health, cheerful obedience, and sound mind of each of its members for its own cohesion and the efficacy of its work. Followers of Benedict were blessed with his common sense and knowledge of the practicalities of living together in community, laced together in essential ways by the "work of God," the essential task of all religious. The abbot, the first among the community, has even greater responsibilities than the brothers, and, like a parent, is much more liable to serious accountability if his charges fail in their tasks or in their adherence to the *Rule*. It was the principal function of every Benedictine monastery to serve God through its regular pattern of worship, for which regular, moderate, and ordered community life was most important. By way of exchange, the daily round of worship afforded monastic clerics a rich education in Scripture (especially but not limited to the psalms), stability of life, and the opportunity to pray for others.

A fitting postscript to this account of Benedict's *Rule* lies with the Emperor Charlemagne, who asked that the version of the *Rule* kept at Monte Cassino, supposedly Benedict's autograph copy, should be copied and disseminated widely throughout his empire. This fact points out the emperor's interest in standardization of religious practice, and the same interest in returning to the best sources possible for widespread dissemination, ideas to which this chapter will shortly return.

[30] RB Chap. 73.

An enormous expansion in the ritual surrounding public worship has already been mentioned, and theologians of the time were quick to ascribe symbolic and mystical significance to many of its elements. In his *Libri officiales*, Amalarius of Metz (d. 851) provides explanations of the ritual that in some cases appear to be allegorical. Elsewhere they are meant to remind the viewer of certain principles of faith or belief, in some way linking action with doctrine. Amalarius refers to the altar (on which are placed the Gospels) variously as Jerusalem (from which the word of the Lord comes, see Isaiah 6:64) or the body of Christ himself "in whom are the words of the Gospel." The candles which precede the Gospel in procession represent the Law and the Prophets, the two forms of divine teaching which antedate the Gospel. By consequence the extinguishing of the candles at the end of the procession show that it is only the Gospel that remains to teach and govern, the Law and Prophets having been superseded. The smoke from the thurible, which also precedes the Gospel in procession, represents the good done by Christ before the good news was proclaimed. More predictably, the high place from which the Gospel is read represents its authority.

With the substantial elaboration of public rites and a concomitant diminution in the functional role of lay worshippers, increasing attention was paid to the nature and function of the worship itself, especially focusing on the minute understanding of the eucharistic sacrifice and the question of precisely how Christ was present in the sacrament of his body and blood under the forms of bread and wine. These were discussions which the Protestant reformers would have nearly a thousand years later, when it was again necessary to enquire into what the Eucharist properly represented. Much attention was spent on the Real Presence of Christ in the elements, leading eventually (in later years) to the doctrine of transubstantiation, but also creating a devotion relating to the elevation of the just-consecrated elements.

Every supposition was up for debate. The theologian Paschasius Radbertus of Corbie (d. 865), wrote that "Nothing is possible outside the will of God . . . therefore let no man be moved from this body and blood of Christ which in a mystery are true flesh and true blood since the Creator so willed it."[31] This being true, it remained a mystery why the consecrated elements continued to look and taste like bread and wine. "If you think of it inwardly," wrote Ratramnus, monk of Corbie, "it is now to the minds of believers not the liquid of Christ's blood, and when tasted, it has flavour; when looked at, it has appearance; and when smelled, it is proved to be such. [Thus] it is clear that bread and wine are Christ's body and blood in a figurative sense."[32] Berengarius of Tours, writing in 1059, recanted a similarly symbolic view of the eucharistic species by affirming that "the bread and wine which are placed on the altar are after consecration not only a Sacrament but also the real body and blood of our Lord Jesus Christ, and that with the senses not only by way of the Sacrament but in reality these are held and broken by the hands of the priests and are crushed by the teeth of the faithful."[33]

Devotion to the body and blood of Christ, truly made present in the consecratory act of the Mass, was such that from the fourth century onward, an increasing number of the faithful did not receive the elements every time they attended the Eucharist, since if they received Christ in a state of sin they would be condemned (in the spirit of 1 Corinthians 11:27-32). Their "spiritual communion" was the compromise. This choice was increasingly justified by doctrine: in the twelfth century there were extensive discussions of the nature of the sacraments which eventually led to favoring spiritual communion or union with the divine—'substituting another devotion'—rather than receiving the elements. The Fourth Lateran Council finally codified the obligations of lay Christians in 1215: it decreed that the faithful should attend confession and receive communion at least once a year, at Easter. This meant that for the

[31] "The Lord's Body and Blood I," in *Early Medieval Theology*, Library of Christian Classics 9, trans. George E. McCracken and Allen Cabaniss (London: SCM Press, 1957), 94.

[32] "Christ's Body and Blood X," in *Early Medieval Theology*, Library of Christian Classics 9, trans. George E. McCracken and Allen Cabaniss (London: SCM Press, 1957), 120–21.

[33] "Recantation," in *A History of the Doctrine of the Holy Eucharist*, trans. Darwell Stone (London: Longmans, 1909), I, 247.

rest of the year, the breaking of the bread within the eucharistic prayer was purely a symbolic gesture, and the richer gesture of a shared meal in which the elements are distributed to the faithful was also relegated to symbolism. Consequently the faithful, who might at one time have brought gifts of bread and wine to be offered at Mass and consecrated, no longer contributed to the service in this way. The form of the rite—priest-centred, dramatic, and closed to lay contributions—had thereby influenced the way the Eucharist was understood to function, and perhaps the reverse might be seen to be true in a cyclic relationship between function and form as ideas were received, reflected in worship, and reiterated.

LITURGY AND INFLUENCE: CHARLEMAGNE'S CONTRIBUTION

We have already seen how the liturgy of the church in Rome was recorded in lavish and detailed accounts of the ceremonies and the talents and actions of the performing forces. The Roman Rite was seen as the foremost and most profitably imitable of all the Western Christian liturgies, not only because it emanated from the seat of the church and was celebrated by the pope and his retinue, but also because it was well attested, being frequently visited and remarked upon by pilgrims and travelers. But Roman liturgy was one of several dialects which enjoyed simultaneous use: throughout Gaul the Gallican Rite was dominant; Milan used the Ambrosian Rite (so named for Ambrose of Milan, although he may have had nothing to do with it); the Spanish employed the Mozarabic or Visigothic Rite; and various parts of the British Isles employed the Celtic Rite, which stemmed from the Christian outposts in the Celtic countries.

By the ninth century, this plurality of liturgical practice, emphasizing the value of local tradition and the independence of the identity and dominion of the ancient regional churches, did not escape the standardizing eye of the new Holy Roman Emperor. Charlemagne had been crowned emperor and Augustus by Pope Leo III on Christmas Day in the year 800, and he hoped to make worship across his empire as uniform, and as close to the practice of Rome, as possible. This connects well with the claim of his biographer Einhard who wrote that, as *patricius Romanus*, protector of the temporal interests of the church's seat at Rome, "throughout his whole reign he considered nothing more important than to re-establish the ancient authority of the city of Rome by his care and by his influence . . . to beautify and enrich it out of his own store above all other churches."[34] This wish may be put down to his own political aspiration for hegemony and the need to be the arbiter of all things. If this is true, it very much demonstrates that Charlemagne and his court understood the important role that local, long-established liturgies played in the sustenance of identity, and the fact that they, like other laws and customs, needed to reflect the wider character of the one Holy Roman Empire. Charlemagne's first visit to Rome in 774 was a matter of great civic ceremony and grandeur, and as he was lauded by state and church alike. Seeds were doubtless sown for a future desire to see Rome's own rituals and traditions spread throughout his realms, including the lands of the un-Christianized Saxons whom he had compelled to accept baptism.

Charlemagne's biographers were careful to represent him as a man of education and, importantly, of great devotion to the service of the church, and with an informed interest in matters liturgical and musical. The courtier Einhard notes that in addition to being a scholar of all the liberal arts, Charlemagne "learned Latin well enough to pray in it as much as in his own native language," a skill which may have been rather beyond many clergy of the period.[35] Throughout his life he attended the morning and evening Offices as well as Mass and Matins, and "especially concerned that everything done in the church should be done with the greatest dignity. . . . He corrected the discipline of reading and singing most carefully, for he was skilled in both. But he himself never read publicly and would only sing in a low voice with the rest of the congregation."[36] These last details, hagiographical in character, again remind the reader that this king was far more talented than

[34] Einhard and Notker the Stammerer, *Two Lives of Charlemagne* (Henceforth TLC), trans. David Ganz (London: Penguin Classics, 2008), 37.

[35] Einhard, TLC, 36.

[36] Ibid., 37. Other hagiographical allusions include the portents of Charlemagne's death including a bridge burn to a cinder, shooting stars, and

many clerics at the skills of worship, simultaneously complimenting Charlemagne and commending the skills he possessed.

Charlemagne's other biographer, Notker (Balbulus) of St. Gall, wrote his Deeds of Charlemagne about seventy years after the emperor's death. Although his main source seems to have been Einhard, Notker nevertheless includes some colorful stories about Charlemagne's liturgical knowledge and prowess. On one occasion when a cleric, hung over after a night of excess, failed to appear at Matins when he was to sing one of the responsories, a "poor and low spirited" monk took the initiative to attempt to sing it after Charlemagne, surprised by the absence, ordered "Let someone sing" when no other member of the choir volunteered. When his attempt ran into difficulties the other clerics tried to stop him, but Charlemagne allowed him to continue, and later rewarded him generously.[37] The emperor was also fond of spontaneously choosing the readers of lessons, so that it was necessary for all the clerics to know which lessons were to be read and to prepare them beautifully. Consequently "everyone in his palace was an excellent reader, even if they did not understand what they read. No one from outside . . . dared to enter his choir unless he could read and chant." Indeed, "No clerk could stay with him, or even come into his presence, unless he was skilled in reading and chanting."[38] Despite this, there is also a story of a liturgically incompetent visiting cleric who, not knowing the proper form, "tried to imitate the behavior of someone singing as best he could." Charlemagne, ignoring the mirth and ridicule of the rest of the choir, thanked the visitor for his efforts sincerely and paid him for his trouble.[39] Again and again Charlemagne's familiarity with the liturgy, even greater than that of his retinue, is celebrated, and its importance to the emperor helps to indicate the importance Notker accorded to worship in the life of the court and consequently of the empire.

"frequent eclipses of the sun and moon and a dark spot . . . on the sun for seven days" (Einhard, 40).

[37] Ibid., 59.

[38] Ibid., 60, 99.

[39] Ibid., 61.

The desire to reproduce the best traditions of Rome in worship are also colorfully recorded in Notker's *Deeds*. "Charles the tireless lover of divine service" regretted that all the regions of his dominion "differed from one another in divine worship, that is, in the modulation of chant." He asked Pope Stephen to send him twelve clerics who were skilled in chant, who would be able to teach the Frankish realms the authentic Roman practices. But the clerics, "being like all Greeks and Romans always full of envy of the fame of the Franks," conspired to ensure each of them taught differently "in as false a manner as they could invent" in each of the largest cities. When Charlemagne visited each of these cities in turn he recognized the musical differences and betrayed the malicious clerics to the Pope who suggested that two of Charlemagne's own retinue be dispatched to Rome to be trained there, and to return and teach more authentically the Roman chant.[40]

Charlemagne's interest in liturgy was coupled with an interest in the deliberations of church councils, including on the matter of the Adoptionist heresy (the belief that Jesus was adopted as God's son, a heresy that had been rejected hundreds of years before). If Notker's evidence, along with other attestations of Charlemagne's interest in chant, are to be accepted, we see in his program of Romanization of the Frankish people a real value accorded to worship as a guarantor of identity and association. Here again, worship is not so much a political tool as both a method and a goal of the Romanization of the Holy Roman Empire that had begun before Charlemagne's own time, although anecdotally (as discussed above) the emperor had a surprising degree of liturgical literacy. The emperor had asked for an exemplar of the Roman practice which could be copied throughout his domains, and Pope Hadrian sent a Gregorian sacramentary, the so-called "Hadrianum," produced in the 730s for the purpose. The Hadrianum, though authentically papal, was missing many of its contents, particularly for particular occasions that required special proper forms. The scholar

[40] One of the manuscripts of the *Deeds* records that the Roman chant had been successfully encouraged at St. Gall, Notker's own monastery.

Benedict of Aniane was tasked with interpolating some of the existing Gallican material with the texts of Hadrian's sacramentary.

Charlemagne's proactive attitude in matters concerning liturgy was not, of course, restricted to his own household. In 789 he issued an order to all clergy insisting that the Gallican chant was to be thoroughly expunged, to be replaced with Roman chant as his father Pepin had ordered; this order was repeated in the synod of 803 at Aachen, when Charlemagne also enjoined the assembled bishops to establish or support schools for the teaching of chant.

The hybridized Romano-Gallican liturgy, which had been developed for use around the Frankish kingdoms, eventually won out as the dominant family of texts and music for worship in Western Europe, supplemented with local adaptations. This in itself would demand a strong recognition of Charlemagne as a key source of liturgical change, but it is also important to identify what an important role he accorded the practice and concept of worship for political aims, for the support of Rome and St. Peter's as the foremost liturgical models, and for their rising to the apex of the Western church. Another part of the cross-fertilization of rites was the emergence of practices previously associated with the Celtic churches, especially forms of penance and confession.

Charlemagne's use of liturgy as a source of and catalyst for temporal and political power was far from unique. After the Norman Conquest, the Anglo-Saxon liturgy that had been used in England was replaced with the Norman pattern familiar to the clerics who rapidly took on positions of authority in their new environment. Equally, the tenth-century Cluniac reform produced an increasingly florid and unceasing liturgical timetable within the new monasteries associated with the first community at Cluny, monasteries allied in their patterns of worship to the mother house. The reforms of Gregory VII also sought to consolidate power and jurisdiction in Rome. The liturgy in the early and High Middle Ages was a powerful tool for the exercise of influence.

CHAPTER 6

The Time of Jesus and the Early Church

> *Go therefore and make disciples of all nations, baptizing them in the name of the Father and of the Son and of the Holy Spirit, and teaching them to obey everything that I have commanded you. And remember, I am with you always, to the end of the age.*
>
> —Matthew 28:19-20

Jesus's final words in the Gospel according to Matthew, addressed to his disciples and sometimes known as the "Great Commission," offer a very clear motivation for action to the early Christian. Some of the ways in which these commands were realized are expressed elsewhere in Scripture, but the wider expression of the activities and beliefs of the earliest times of the church requires a fuller exploration, including an examination of a wider number of Scriptural points and other influences on contemporaneous culture. It might be thought that the earliest practitioners of Christian worship had fewer historical pressures on their beliefs and practices than later adherents might seem to have. In reality, there were undoubted influences from Jewish, Greco-Roman, and pagan culture.

Throughout Christian history there have been many points at which Scriptural (or very early) institution of certain teachings has been cited as the key inspiration—and sometimes the necessary condition—for their validity and effectiveness. Many times, especially in the debates about the number and nature of sacraments (but also elsewhere), a Scriptural model has been pointed to as the critical point of institution. The period immediately following the life of Jesus is the natural focus of interest for a study of liturgical practices that have long been understood to have been established by Christ in the case of the sacraments and (at least in recent times) organized explicitly around the habits of the early church.

Yet in the earliest days of Christian activity the followers of Jesus were a very small minority in a hostile world. They met in secret without public recognition of their faith and the question of how their prayer life could have been sustained must be considered in light of the fact that the personal faith of practicing Christians, in these very difficult conditions in which they were in fact persecuted criminals, must have been very strong.

WHY WORSHIP?

In Scriptural accounts and in the earliest documentary records, the worship of the followers of Jesus, above all, fulfilled a community-building function. This was for several linked reasons, highlighted in the second chapter of the Acts of the Apostles: "Those who welcomed [Peter's] message were baptized. . . . They devoted themselves to the apostles' teaching and fellowship, to the breaking of bread and to the prayers" (Acts 2:41-42). The rites of initiation through baptism were celebrated in the wider community, where new converts were received as they had been in the time of Christ's ministry. The teachings of Christ, received through the apostles, were taught and disseminated through retelling in the assembly (an important task for a fringe religion, as it was), and the recollection of Christ's breaking of bread with his disciples was enacted, although the precise form it took before the earliest documents is not clear. There were certainly correspondences with the sacrificial communion-offering of the Jewish Passover meal, as well as with earlier forms of table fellowship from the Classical world. It is also clear that with respect to public prayer, there was some inheritance of models from synagogue worship, with which the earliest Christians would have been familiar. The establishment of authentically Christian forms, albeit inspired by these antecedents, would have been a step toward independence and legitimization in the eyes of the believers.

WHAT HAPPENED?

There are very few records that depict with any great detail the earliest Christian forms of worship or the character of the public prayer of the church. We can say with certainty that it was attuned to the cultural principles of the wider community in which Christians operated. In addition to what it owed to the teachings and ministry of Jesus himself, the form, as well as the concept, of worship drew richly from pre-existent Jewish formulations (these, as well as the Hebrew Scriptures, were held in common). As the number of observant Christians grew, the community could not have existed in "one place" as attested in Acts; and because of the decentralized nature of the church (it met in houses rather than in dedicated buildings and was under the control of local elders rather than centralized, authoritative, hierarchical control), it was unlikely that one Christian community would worship in the same way as another. Some of the difficulties associated with small, independent communities are described in the letters of Paul to various churches.

SCRIPTURAL REFERENCES

In a scholarly climate accustomed to the perceived veracity of historical, empirically proven documentary sources, the complete accuracy of the Scriptural account for worship can be rather easily cast into doubt, not least because of what it chooses to include and exclude from the story. For our purposes, however, it should be kept clearly in mind that the generations that followed the witnesses to Jesus took the Scriptural basis for their activities seriously. As the Scriptures were the prime influence for subsequent developments, they need to be considered carefully here as well.

THE EUCHARIST

Numerous depictions of the Last Supper show Jesus and his disciples seated around a long table, often with implements such as chalices familiar from the Christian reenactment of the actions. These images help to associate the acts of Christ directly with the rites of the Eucharist. This is evidently part of the function of the eucharistic action, associating gestures rich in symbolism with the Scripturally attested event, but it makes the development of the rite rather more difficult to trace. The "breaking of bread," as it emerged and was practiced in the early church, did not emerge fully formed and unprecedented by Christ's institution. The ritual of blessing and sharing food and fellowship needs to be presented within the wider context of the Hellenistic meal-sharing tradition as well as the Jewish practice of blessings before and after meals and particularly the symbolism and memory-making which are vital to the shared meal at Passover.

In the ancient world, meals, taken by the wealthy in rooms with couches for reclining, were an opportunity to gain or affirm influence, or to offer hospitality to clients or patrons. The expression of table-fellowship extended to persons who were of lower social standing than the patron, although it is likely that people who were not social equals did not eat together and sometimes did not even eat the same food. In this way, connections between individuals, and the interactions of constituents of a community, were fostered through sharing of food and drink, the latter dedicated to the gods through prayer and the pouring out of libations.

Equally, the Jewish convention of blessing wine and offering prayers at the ends of meals (*berakah*), attested by among other sources the meal-blessings of the Qumran community, offers another set of customs surrounding mealtimes which has been aligned with the acts of Jesus at the Last Supper. But it is not clear to what degree these prayers and blessings had been formalized before the promulgation of the *Mishnah*, the first collection of rabbinic sayings, which gave these rites definition. It also must be remembered that as a Jew, Jesus defied a number of the conventions relating to meals: he ate with tax collectors and sinners, people who were inappropriate dinner companions (Mark 2:16; Luke 5:30); his disciples ate and drank, unlike the disciples of John and of the Pharisees (Luke 5:33); the disciples collected corn to eat on the Sabbath (Matt 12:1); and they ate without washing their hands (Matt 15:2, Mark 7:2). On each of these occasions, Jesus rebuffs criticism by citing the fulfilment of the Law, and the reader is forced to consider the implications of his actions. Radical table fellowship allows meals to be shared with all. The feeding of crowds with blessed and broken bread prefigure the commission, echoed in the various accounts of the institution of the Eucharist at the Last Supper, to "do this in remembrance of me": to remind the faithful of Christ, his death and resurrection.

The breaking of bread at Emmaus is the means by which the disciples recognize Jesus, and in the years following his ascension the act must have been a potent reminder: the second chapter of the Acts of the Apostles recounts how the apostles and new converts alike came together in fellowship with "the breaking of bread and the prayers." New Christians "day by day . . . spent much time together in the temple, they broke bread at home [in the Authorized Version, 'from house to house'] and ate their food with glad and generous hearts, praising God and having the goodwill of all the people" (Acts 2:42-47). What this breaking of bread might have looked and sounded like we do not know, although it almost certainly took a variable form that may have taken cues from the blessing of food familiar to the Jewish followers of Jesus. It may not have slavishly followed the gestures and pattern of the Last Supper precisely, despite many efforts to link the early historical record to the Scriptural account or, alternatively with Gregory Dix, to the fourfold ritual actions of "taking," "blessing," "breaking," and "giving" which are purportedly found in all ritual patterns of the Eucharist.[1]

Similarly, just because the association of Jesus's own body and blood with the bread and wine of the shared meal did become a commonplace, it is not necessarily helpful to think that this was automatically the case from the start; rather, the rite as it developed is a condensation of the imperative from Jesus to "do this in remembrance of me," the condensation of the recalled actions of the Last Supper and the numerous contemporaneous mealtime conventions. The "institution of the Eucharist" and "the Last Supper" may be one and the same, but there is nothing to suggest there is a recognizable, direct line of textual or ritual descent from Jesus, through the early church, down to the present.

We have already noted the similarity of the blessing of the bread and wine to Jewish rituals surrounding food, and in no circumstance are these rituals more prominent than at the Passover, the observance of which marks the salvation of the Israelites and the

[1] Gregory Dix, *The Shape of the Liturgy* (London: Dacre Press, 1945), 48–102.

judgment the Lord visited on Egypt through the death of all firstborn children. The Lord commanded Moses and Aaron to tell each household of their people to sacrifice a lamb:

> You shall keep it until the fourteenth day of this month; then the whole assembled congregation of Israel shall slaughter it at twilight. They shall take some of the blood and put it on the two doorposts and the lintel of the houses in which they eat it. They shall eat the lamb that same night; they shall eat it roasted over the fire with unleavened bread and bitter herbs. (Exod 12:6-8)

The sprinkling of blood on the lintel and door-posts of the houses was recognized by the Lord as a sign of their faith and obedience, and was in future to be obeyed as a commemoration of the salvation of Israel from Egypt by the Lord's hand:

> You shall observe this rite as a perpetual ordinance for you and your children. When you come to the land that the Lord will give you, as he has promised, you shall keep this observance. And when your children ask you, "What do you mean by this observance?" you shall say, "It is the passover sacrifice to the Lord, for he passed over the houses of the Israelites in Egypt, when he struck down the Egyptians but spared our houses." And the people bowed down and worshipped. (Exod 12:24-27)

The Passover lambs are among the different types of offering made to God in the Hebrew Bible, but unlike them, most of the other sacrifices were burnt so that nothing remained. The lambs, after slaughter, were to be taken home, their blood used as a sign, their flesh to be roasted and eaten by the households who sacrificed them. In a sense the Israelites themselves are sharing in the sacrifice with the Lord; this type of sacrifice can be termed a "communion-offering."

In the Gospels of Matthew, Mark, and Luke, the Last Supper is a Passover meal taken with the disciples (i.e., Matt 26:17). In the Gospel of John (in which there is no narrative of the Passover) the imagery remains because Jesus dies on the cross at the time when, in the Temple, the lambs are being taken to be sacrificed. The appropriateness of this parallel is not lost in John, where Jesus is also described as the "Lamb of God" (John 1:29, 36). The other three Gospel accounts, as well as the account of the institution of the Eucharist in Paul's first letter to the Corinthians, demonstrate relative consistency:

> While they were eating, Jesus took a loaf of bread, and after blessing it he broke it, gave it to the disciples, and said, "Take, eat; this is my body." Then he took a cup, and after giving thanks he gave it to them, saying, "Drink from it, all of you; for this is my blood of the covenant, which is poured out for many for the forgiveness of sins. I tell you, I will never again drink of this fruit of the vine until that day when I drink it new with you in my Father's kingdom." (Matt 26:26-30)
>
> While they were eating, he took a loaf of bread, and after blessing it he broke it, gave it to them, and said, "Take; this is my body." Then he took a cup, and after giving thanks he gave it to them, and all of them drank from it. He said to them, "This is my blood of the covenant, which is poured out for many. Truly I tell you, I will never again drink of the fruit of the vine until that day when I drink it new in the kingdom of God." (Mark 14:22-26)
>
> When the hour came, he took his place at the table, and the apostles with him. He said to them, "I have eagerly desired to eat this Passover with you before I suffer; for I tell you, I will not eat it until it is fulfilled in the kingdom of God." Then he took a cup, and after giving thanks he said, "Take this and divide it among yourselves; for I tell you that from now on I will not drink of the fruit of the vine until the kingdom of God comes." Then he took a loaf of bread, and when he had given thanks, he broke it and gave it to them, saying, "This is my body, which is given for you. Do this in remembrance of me." And he did the same with the cup after supper, saying, "This cup that is poured out for you is the new covenant in my blood. But see, the one who betrays me is with me, and his hand is on the table. For the Son of Man is going as it has been determined, but woe to that one by whom he is betrayed!" (Luke 22:14-22)
>
> For I received from the Lord what I also handed on to you, that the Lord Jesus on the night when he was betrayed took a loaf of bread, and when he had given thanks, he broke it and said, "This is my

> body that is for you. Do this in remembrance of me." In the same way he took the cup also, after supper, saying, "This cup is the new covenant in my blood. Do this, as often as you drink it, in remembrance of me." For as often as you eat this bread and drink the cup, you proclaim the Lord's death until he comes. (1 Cor 11:23-26)

The form of sharing for the bread and wine may not have been fixed, but there was also a growing separation of the sharing of bread and wine according to Christ's command from the feeding of material hunger, perhaps through the expanded resources necessary to supply a substantive meal for a growing number of the faithful, or perhaps as a consequence of the illegal nature of the act, or more possibly the growing significance of the bread and wine as representing something other than physical nourishment.

The *Didache* (Teaching of the Twelve Apostles), written as early as the late first century, is one of the earliest sources for information about the table fellowship of the earliest Christians. Chapters 9 and 10 of the *Didache* concern the Eucharist. In giving thanks for wine and bread, the president thanks God the Father for "the holy vine" and "the life and knowledge" revealed through Jesus, praying that "as this [bread] . . . was scattered over the hills and then was brought together and made one, so let your Church be brought together from the ends of the earth into your kingdom." The closing prayer at the end of the meal thanks God for his sacred Name, and for the knowledge and faith expressed through Christ, through whom God gave "spiritual food and drink and eternal life."[2] The *Didache* also enjoins Christians to "break bread and give thanks" on the Lord's day, having confessed their sins. While there are separate blessings for the bread and wine, the form of these prayers differs in at least one significant way from later rites surrounding the Eucharist in that there is no reminder of the activities of the Last Supper, nor of the redemptive power of the meal. There are also some similarities between the rite in the *Didache* and the *Birkat ha-mazon*, or Jewish meal-blessing, which may point to its use particularly by Jewish Christians.

[2] *Didache* in PEER, chaps. 9 and 10, 22–23.

A clear expression of the spiritual function of the Eucharist, in the breaking of bread, is witnessed in a letter to the Ephesians of Ignatius of Antioch, writing about 115 AD. He writes that the broken loaf "is the medicine of immortality, and the antidote which wards off death but yields continuous life in union with Jesus Christ."[3]

Justin Martyr, who was writing in the middle of the second century AD, supplies a relatively comprehensive account of the action surrounding the blessing and sharing of bread and wine. In his *First Apology* he gives a very clear sense of the different components of the rite. Following (in this case) a baptism and the exchange of a kiss, the congregation offer up bread, wine, and water. Next, the president of the celebration offers praise to the Trinity and prayers of thanksgiving for being deemed worthy of sharing in the meal. These prayers seem to have been extemporized or were at the least quite variable. All the faithful say "Amen," translated as "So be it." The bread and wine are distributed by the deacons (who are the representatives of the bishop) to the congregation, and also to those who were not present at the celebration. Another section of the *Apology* describes eucharistic action this way: "on the day called Sunday an assembly is held in one place of all who live in town or country [notable for its inclusivity], and the records of the apostles or the writings of the prophets are read as time allows."[4] A discourse from the president follows, and then prayer, the bringing of bread and wine, praise and thanksgiving (prayed by the president "to the best of his ability"), the Amen, and the distribution. Despite the formulation, it is not clear when this service might have taken place: possibly a Saturday night, not necessarily separated from a meal. It is worth pointing out that Justin's account implies that the president's part may be extemporized, rather than adhering to a fixed form. The reference to a sequence of readings and prayers preceding the Eucharist may once again relate to Jewish precedent, and agrees well with the account

[3] "Letters," in *Early Christian Fathers*, Library of Christian Classics, trans. Cyril C. Richardson (London: SCM Press, 1953), 93.

[4] *First Apology*, in PEER, 29.

of Jesus's interactions with the disciples on the road to Emmaus. Justin's text illustrates one contemporary attitude to the eucharistic meal:

> We do not receive these things as common bread or common drink; but just as our Saviour Jesus Christ, being incarnate by the word of God, took flesh and blood for our salvation, so too we have been taught that the food over which thanks have been given by a word of prayer which is from him, (the food) from which our flesh and blood are fed by transformation, is both the flesh and blood of that incarnate Jesus.[5]

Similarly, Ambrose of Milan (circa 390) contemplates the nature of the consecration, and the agent by which it operates:

> This bread is bread before the sacramental words; when the consecration has taken place, from being bread it becomes the flesh of Christ . . . How can that which is bread be the body of Christ? By consecration . . . The priest no longer uses his own words, but he uses the words of Christ. Therefore the word of Christ makes this sacrament.[6]

It is not clear how these comments were understood, although they are almost certainly not portents of the doctrine of the Real Presence of Christ.

Another key text for insight into the eucharistic practices of early Christianity is the *Apostolic Tradition*, probably dating from the fourth century and formerly attributed to Hippolytus of Rome. This document shares with other contemporary documents a clear narrative of the institution of the Eucharist by Jesus (*anamnesis*) as well as an expression of Christ's divine birth and life, and the unambiguous statement that he suffered "that he might destroy death and break the bonds of the devil, and tread down hell, and shine

[5] Ibid., 29.

[6] Ambrose, "On the Sacraments IV, 14," in Darwell Stone, *A History of the Doctrine of the Holy Eucharist* vol. 1, 81–82.

upon the righteous."[7] The *Apostolic Tradition* also includes the *epiclesis*, the prayer for the sending down of the Holy Spirit upon the offering, and prayer for the fruits of the redemption of the faithful. Later writers like Cyril of Jerusalem and John Chrysostom report prayers which ask God to send the Spirit on the bread and wine to "make" them the body and blood, "changing it by your holy Spirit, Amen."[8]

As time went by, an increased emphasis on the redemptive power of Christ's sacrifice, memorialized in a rite which was becoming progressively more formal, full of symbolism, and rich in personal significance for those who attended it, must have meant an atmosphere of increased solemnity and promising a propensity for personal devotion and, progressively, a separation of the symbolic act from a realistic meal. There had been a custom, witnessed in Justin and in another early Christian author, Tertullian, of taking the bread (and sometimes the wine) to those who were not able to attend the celebration in person. It would seem that this sharing began with life-sustaining amounts of sustenance conveyed to the poor, a charitable practice, but as the bread and wine became more closely associated with a ritual than with a meal, the function of this extended distribution became an opportunity for non-attendees to partake of the shared sacrifice.

The legalization of Christianity across the Roman Empire encouraged the structures and texts of liturgy, couched in symbolic action and dramatic stories which had sustained the Christian people in the days of their persecution, to become a teaching room for new generations of believers. Through the opening up of Christian practice to the public and, subsequently, to a much greater number of professed faithful (though the gumption required for conversion to an illegal religion must have been rather stronger), Christian worship began to be attended by a much wider cross section of the population. An attendant increase in solemnity, grandeur, and ceremonial was intended at least in part to inculcate appropriately reverent sentiments from the congregation. Cyril of

[7] PEER, 34–35.

[8] *The Liturgy of St. John Chrysostom*, in PEER, 133.

Jerusalem shows new converts how to receive the Eucharist in the palm of their hand: "Make your left hand a throne for your right, since your right hand is about to welcome a king. . . . For to lose any of [the bread] is clearly like losing part of your own body."[9] The worthiness of the faithful to receive had been commented upon by Paul:

> Whoever, therefore, eats the bread or drinks the cup of the Lord in an unworthy manner will be answerable for the body and blood of the Lord. Examine yourselves, and only then eat of the bread and drink of the cup. For all who eat and drink without discerning the body, eat and drink judgment against themselves. (1 Cor 11:27-29)

Justin Martyr echoes similar sentiments:

> No one may partake of it unless he is convinced of the truth of our teaching, and has been cleansed with the washing for forgiveness of sins and regeneration, and lives as Christ handed down.[10]

Those who deemed themselves unworthy to communicate, or who had failed to amend improper behavior, were encouraged to make their confession before returning, but this had the predictable effect of discouraging them from communicating at all. Because this practice came to be accepted by the church, members of the congregation who would otherwise have been communicating began to see the celebration of the Eucharist as complete within itself without their participation, and the offering of the service by the priest complete without their own response to it. The ritual of the service, intended to draw in viewers to the importance of their own contribution, as well as to teach and to represent, became an occasion for unengaged devotion. This was a state of affairs which stood a long way off from the shared meal of Scripture or the

[9] *Mystagogical Catechesis of Cyril of Jerusalem*, 5:21–22, cited in Paul Bradshaw, *The Search for the Origins of Christian Worship*, 2nd ed. (London: SPCK, 2002), 216.

[10] *First Apology* 66.1, in PEER, 29.

earlier accounts. A very rapid dissociation of the abstracted rite of the Eucharist from the sharing of a meal was not far away.

> The cup of blessing that we bless, is it not a sharing in the blood of Christ? The bread that we break, is it not a sharing in the body of Christ? Because there is one bread, we who are many are one body, for we all partake of the one bread. You cannot drink the cup of the Lord and the cup of demons. You cannot partake of the table of the Lord and the table of demons. (1 Cor 10:16-17, 21)

The "sharing in the blood of Christ," then, was in no way a literal one, but a memorial alone, and to "partake of the one bread" was separated from any act of eating whatever, whether of a full meal or of a symbolic amount.

DAILY PUBLIC PRAYER

As with blessings at mealtimes, early Christian practice had much to build upon in Jewish temple and synagogue practices. Daily sacrifices were ordained by God for the Jewish priesthood:

> Now this is what you shall offer on the altar: two lambs a year old regularly each day. One lamb you shall offer in the morning, and the other lamb you shall offer in the evening. (Exod 29:38-39)

The Psalms are also a source of texts on prayer which would have had resonance for early Christians, but it is not clear how these produced an effect on actual practice:

> Evening and morning and at noon
> I utter my complaint and moan,
> and he will hear my voice.
> At midnight I rise to praise you,
> because of your righteous ordinances.
> . . .
> Seven times a day I praise you
> for your righteous ordinances. (Ps 119:62, 164)

> Let my prayer be counted as incense before you,
> and the lifting up of my hands as an evening sacrifice. (Ps 141:2)

It was Jewish custom to pray two or three times a day, although authorities differ on the precise timings. The *Didache*, similarly, does not indicate the timing of prayer, although it specifies the Lord's Prayer as a suitable text to be used. Clement of Alexandria and Tertullian suggest the third, sixth, and ninth hours of the day. Clement compares the raising of prayer to God with physical action. He writes:

> prayer is . . . to speak more boldly, to converse with God. Though whispering . . . and not opening the lips, we speak in silence, yet we cry inwardly. For God hears all the inward converse. So also we raise the head and lift the hands to heaven, and set the feet in motion at the closing utterance of the prayer, following the eagerness of the spirit directed towards the intellectual essence; and endeavouring to abstract the body from the earth, along with the discourse, raising the soul aloft.[11]

In the *Apostolic Tradition*, seven occasions for prayer were encouraged: in the morning, to commit the day to God; at the third hour, when Christ was nailed to the cross; at the sixth hour, when Christ was on the cross and darkness fell; at the ninth hour, when his side was pierced; before bedtime; around midnight, for "at that hour all creation is still for a moment, to praise the Lord"; and at cockcrow, recalling the denial of Christ. There began to be an imperative especially for clergy to be present. The priests and deacons are enjoined to assemble together and "teach those who are in the church, and in this way, when they have prayed, let each one go to the work which falls to him." All were to come diligently for instruction, and if none were to be available, they were to "take up a holy book and read in it sufficiently what seems to [one] to bring profit."[12] The theologian Origen, writing in the third century, points out that to "pray without ceasing" (1 Thess 5:17), fitting prayers must be combined with fitting actions, and that the actions

[11] Clement of Alexandria, *Stromata or Miscellanies* VII.7, trans. William Wilson, *Ante-Nicene Fathers* II, 534.

[12] "Apostolic Tradition," in G.J. Cuming, *Hippolytus: A Text for Students* (Bramcote: Grove Books, 1976), 28–29.

devoted specifically to praise and prayer should be observed "not less than three times every day."[13] Morning and evening prayer were a constant in instructions, and the *Apostolic Constitutions*, a fourth-century document, instructs the bishop to command the people, both clergy and lay, to come to church each day at those times, not forsaking this duty:

> and causing the body of Christ to be without its members or [preferring] the occasions of this life to the word of God, but assemble yourselves together every day, morning and evening, singing psalms and praying in the Lord's house: in the morning saying the sixty-third psalm, and in the evening the hundred and forty-[first], but principally on the Sabbath-day. And on the day of our Lord's resurrection . . . meet more diligently . . . If it be not possible to assemble either in the church or in a house, let everyone by himself sing, and read, and pray, or two or three together.[14]

INITIATION

Followers of Christ were initiated into his body, the church, by means of water baptism, a rite undergone by Jesus and later seen as one of the sacraments instituted by him in the Scriptural records. The accounts of two of the evangelists indicate some reticence on the part of John the Baptist to exercise this ministry of repentance upon Jesus and indeed the desire to be baptized by him instead. The baptism of Christ marks the beginning of his public life and preaching, and the appearance of the Spirit descending like a dove is a sign of God's favor. The four Gospel accounts provide different details, although John uniquely provides the witness of the Baptist himself, as if for the reader's particular benefit:

> Then Jesus came from Galilee to John at the Jordan, to be baptized by him. John would have prevented him, saying, "I need to be baptized by you, and do you come to me?" But Jesus answered him,

[13] Origen, "On Prayer," XII.2, in *Alexandrian Christianity*, Library of Christian Classics, ed. Henry Chadwick and J.E.L. Oulton (London: SCM Press, 1954), 261–62.

[14] *Apostolic Constitutions*, trans. James Donaldson, Ante-Nicene Fathers VII, 422–23.

> "Let it be so now; for it is proper for us in this way to fulfil all righteousness." Then he consented. And when Jesus had been baptized, just as he came up from the water, suddenly the heavens were opened to him and he saw the Spirit of God descending like a dove and alighting on him. And a voice from heaven said, "This is my Son, the Beloved, with whom I am well pleased." (Matt 3:13-17)

> In those days Jesus came from Nazareth of Galilee and was baptized by John in the Jordan. And just as he was coming up out of the water, he saw the heavens torn apart and the Spirit descending like a dove on him. And a voice came from heaven, "You are my Son, the Beloved; with you I am well pleased." (Mark 1:9-11)

> Now when all the people were baptized, and when Jesus also had been baptized and was praying, the heaven was opened, and the Holy Spirit descended upon him in bodily form like a dove. And a voice came from heaven, "You are my Son, the Beloved; with you I am well pleased." (Luke 3:21-22)

> The next day [John] saw Jesus coming towards him and declared, "Here is the Lamb of God who takes away the sin of the world! This is he of whom I said, 'After me comes a man who ranks ahead of me because he was before me.' I myself did not know him; but I came baptizing with water for this reason, that he might be revealed to Israel." And John testified, "I saw the Spirit descending from heaven like a dove, and it remained on him. I myself did not know him, but the one who sent me to baptize with water said to me, 'He on whom you see the Spirit descend and remain is the one who baptizes with the Holy Spirit.' And I myself have seen and have testified that this is the Son of God." (John 1:29-34)

The letter of Paul to the Romans identifies the critical principle of human salvation in Christ, one that provides an enduring image for baptism that has influenced the theological understanding of the rite:

> Do you not know that all of us who have been baptized into Christ Jesus were baptized into his death? Therefore we have been buried with him by baptism into death, so that, just as Christ was raised from the dead by the glory of the Father, so we too might walk in newness of life. (Rom 6:3-5)

Ambrose comments that the baptismal font gives the visual impression of a tomb (and has a similar function),[15] while Augustine, too, remarks that,

> all who attain to [the grace of baptism] die thereby to sin—as [Christ] himself is said to have died to sin because he died in the flesh, that is, "in the likeness of sin"—and they are thereby alive by being reborn in the baptismal font, just as he rose again from the sepulchre.[16]

The "death" is shown by Cyril of Jerusalem to be "but in a figure, but our salvation is in reality."[17] The image of dying to sin and rising through baptism to new life in Christ has been a pervasive one, linked with salvation by Jesus's admonition in John's Gospel that "no one can enter the kingdom of God without being born of water and Spirit" (John 3:5). Baptism is the means by which, using another images, all the members of Christ are united in one body, irrespective of their own particular characteristics: "For in the one Spirit we were all baptized into one body—Jews or Greeks, slaves or free—and we were all made to drink of one Spirit" (1 Cor 12:13). The "Great Commission" in the final chapter of Matthew points to baptism "in the name of the Father and of the Son and of the Holy Spirit," as one of the most important activities of the church, and baptism is mentioned in the Acts of the Apostles when new converts are introduced into the church, memorably in the story of Philip and the eunuch:

> As they were going along the road, they came to some water; and the eunuch said, "Look, here is water! What is to prevent me from being baptized?" He commanded the chariot to stop, and both of them, Philip and the eunuch, went down into the water, and Philip baptized him. (Acts 8:36-38)

[15] Ambrose, "On the Sacraments III.1," in *St. Ambrose 'on the Mysteries' and the Treatise 'on the Sacraments,'* trans. T. Thompson (London: SPCK, 1919), 96.

[16] "Enchiridion XIII," in *Augustine: Confessions and Enchiridion*, trans. A.C. Outler, Library of Christian Classics (London: SCM Press, 1955), 365.

[17] Cyril of Jerusalem, "Mystagogical Catechesis," in *St. Cyril of Jerusalem's Lectures on the Christian Sacraments*, ed. F.L. Cross, trans. R.W. Church (London: SPCK, 1960), II.5.

The *Didache* provides instructions for baptism, specifying that the candidate "and any others who can" should fast in advance of the rite, and that the water used should be running water where possible. It does not give very specific details of *how* the candidate is to be baptized otherwise, except that it is to be done in the name of the Trinity, and that pouring water on the head three times is a suitable alternative to running water. Clement of Alexandria supplied many alternative, descriptive names for baptism by means of explanation, including "gift of grace, enlightenment, perfection, washing . . . by which we are cleansed from the filth of our sins, gift of grace, by which the penalties of our sins are cancelled; enlightenment, through which that holy light which saves us is perceived."[18] Justin Martyr writes that the candidates, having undergone teaching in the faith and confession of their sins, "while we pray and fast along with them," are brought to the water (again not specified). The name of God is invoked, and the candidates are baptized in the name of the Trinity. "This washing," he writes, "is called illumination, since those who learn these things are illumined within."[19] Tertullian further discusses washing, pointing out that "the spirit is in those waters corporally washed, while the flesh is in those same waters spiritually cleansed." He comments that according to individuals' personalities, it can be beneficial to defer baptism (especially the baptism of children and of the unmarried). "So let them come when they are growing up, when they are learning, when they are being taught what they are coming to."[20]

The *Apostolic Tradition* indicates that catechumens are to be carefully questioned to ensure they are coming to faith genuinely and appropriately, and with constancy. Those who have professions not becoming to the faith (such as brothel-keepers, actors, priests of

[18] Clement of Alexandria, "The Teacher, I.vi.26," in *The Early Christian Fathers*, trans. Henry Bettenson (London: Oxford University Press, 1963), 247.

[19] Justin Martyr, "First Apology 61," in *Library of Christian Classics* 1, trans. Edward Rochie Hardy, (London, SCM Press, 1953), 282–83.

[20] Tertullian, "On Baptism" in *Tertullian's Homily on Baptism*, trans. by Ernest Evans (London: SPCK, 1964) art. 18. Recall that Paul comments on the constancy of the unmarried in 1 Corinthians.

other religions, the violent) are rejected. The process of catechesis takes some three years, after which they are exorcised by the bishop and keep vigil. The bishop blesses oils of exorcism and of thanksgiving, the candidates are anointed with the former before going into the water professing their faith, and are baptized, anointed with the oil of thanksgiving, and exit the water to be signed with the same oil again.

The related rite of confirmation has its origins in the fact that priests began to take on the role of the ordinary minister of baptism, replacing the bishop, which was followed some time later by a blessing by the relevant bishop. This change was a result of baptisms taking place at times other than Easter, for instance because infants born at certain times of the year might not survive long enough to be baptized. In northern Europe especially, weather and travel conditions prevented this from happening in short order, and the rites gradually became separated.

In the same way that the end of the persecution of Christians in the early fourth century permitted men and women to join the ranks of the faithful who were perhaps less fervent and tested in their faith, the act of baptism became a commonplace, applied to people who had not undergone a dramatic and illegal conversion, and similarly rather less significant efforts at catechesis were made. Baptism's significance for personal salvation is not forgotten, however, and in practice it was often delayed to a point late in life or close to death, and so some Christians remained "catechumens" awaiting baptism all their lives.

Epilogue

It is a warm afternoon in July, and I am writing these words in the cool quiet of a city center church. From time to time, a visitor comes in and looks around the medieval interior, reordered and redesigned several times over its long history. One caller has even come to look specially at the north aisle designed by George Gilbert Scott. Others walk in and, without pausing, walk straight out. Considerably more faces appear at the door, looking in, than ever cross the threshold. But not all are here as tourists alone: many come in to pray or light a candle, or to spend some time in the peace and stillness of the church.

The reason such church buildings exist was to have places where Christians, as their numbers grew after the years of their persecution, would be able to worship together. But now, as those numbers diminish, churches as physical places, and also as congregations which gather together, are having to re-evaluate their identity. The number of people, of all ages, who walk through the door of the church in a few hours on a weekday afternoon is perhaps surprisingly high, if we consider the undeniably dwindling numbers, on the whole, who attend traditional church gatherings on Sundays, in which Christians meet and participate in forms of worship established through historical precedent.

In my afternoon sitting in church, a steady but small stream of visitors entered, stayed for a while, and then left, each one of them walking over the threshold for his or her own reasons, to sit or pray or think or look at the architecture with independent minds and agendas. This poignant scene may bring to mind the dwindling of church congregations, but in contemplating the fact that significant numbers of people still visit churches, pilgrimage sites, shrines, and other venues generally understood as religious, we are also led to think that even when avowedly attending an organized gathering, people come to church, and have always come to church, for different reasons and with different ways of perceiving the action.

In the preceding chapters we have asked why people in different historical periods and with different conceptions of church, theology, and culture have worshipped, what that worship might have offered to the senses, and, over time, what particular functions public worship played in Christian society. These are, of course, questions which could be asked readily not just of Christians but of any church or religion with an element of corporate fellowship or gathering, and a similarly vast array of explanations, over time, could be amassed as to motivations and principles. But could the same be addressed to a "church" where the common creed is that there is no God and that life in the here and now should be celebrated?

In recent years more than one "church" for self-identified atheists has come into being. These gatherings have been inspired by the "ethical unions" of more than a hundred years ago. Such gatherings took a quasi-liturgical form, but rather than discourse with divinity, members chose to foster a church-like community that provided opportunities for secular self-improvement. One such community, founded in 2013 in London by two stand-up comedians but possessing a serious attitude, has set up in a deconsecrated church. Its defined format, led by a compère, features the singing of songs by those present, who also listen to a secular address. There is time for quiet contemplation, too, within the context of these events. Nick Spencer, a researcher investigating the role of religion in society, writes in the *Guardian*:

> What you see in these modern-day atheist churches is people united by a felt absence of community. I suspect what brings them together is a real desire for community when in a modern, urbanized individualized city like London you can often feel very alone.[1]

It may be a desire for a regular, church-like gathering (an opportunity one does not normally have outside the realm of organized religion) that is behind the success of atheist groups, but the reasons for that desire need to be interrogated. Is it that people

[1] Esther Addley, "No Rest for the Wicked: Atheist Churches Go Forth and Multiply," *The Guardian*, September 14, 2013, p. 13.

without a church affiliation feel more lonely or unfulfilled? Do they seek a home for their "spiritual but not religious" beliefs, one that concurs with the belief system of others so that, in an increasingly individualistic world, there will be a few moments of unanimity and shared purpose? Is there an overbearingly substantial nostalgia for something needed yet apparently from another time? The very existence of "atheist churches" give some indication that, at least for them, "liturgy" is all about fulfilling hopeful ambitions, sharing in community life, and taking part in a communitarian, corporate activity. But these gatherings are not "churches," nor can what they do on a Sunday morning be described as worship for, while it may be celebratory in character or give pause for thought and reflection, it is inwardly directed, like a political conference or an academic seminar. Recall Augustine's definition of a hymn, which very clearly and simply establishes the objective and the form, and especially the addressee, of this particular element of worship: "The praise of God, when sung, is called a hymn." The definition of worship is also one of a necessarily God-directed activity.

This book has tried to illustrate, through words and examples, that there are a multitude of sacramental, cultural, and didactic functions of Christian worship, ways in which its enactment was understood, keyed to particular times and circumstances, in addition to the seemingly simplistic explanation, the main reason why secular communities and sacred ones stand apart: the glorification of God and the sanctification of the faithful. Succeeding chapters have treated the liturgy as a means of solidarity in persecution (the communitarian liturgy of the early church), constancy in practice (establishing the great timetables of prayer in the early Middle Ages, along with liturgy's political influence), grandeur in performance (expressed through the fullest embrace of elaborate rites in the late Middle Ages), edification through transformation (by the Reformers), potency through nostalgia (in the revival of earlier forms by the Liturgical Movement), or growth through community (Vatican II).

Beyond these elements, the principal objective of prayer and praise to God remains. And to explain the necessity or motivation for this supreme and necessary act is, within the Wittgensteinian mythology, to seek and fail to find appropriate words.

Index

Names of the Divine Persons, denominations (i.e., Catholic Church, Anglican Church, Protestant Churches), and references to Reformations are deliberately excluded: see specific concepts.

absolution, 76
Amalarius of Metz, 132
Ambrose of Milan, Saint, 148
Anglo-Catholic (movement in the Church of England), 11–12, 23, 38
Antony of Egypt, Saint, 123–24
Apostolic Tradition (document), 148, 152
atheism: ethical unions, 159
attendance at church, modern, xviii, xix, xxvi, 158–59
Augsburg Confession, 77–78
Augustine of Hippo, Saint, xi, 123–24, 160
Augustinian canons, 98

baptism, 63, 79–80, 140, 147, 153–57
bells, 25, 76, 92
Benedict of Nursia, Saint (Rule of), 97, 120, 121, 126–31
Benedict XVI, Pope, xxviii
Bible, 1, 20, 22–23, 57–58, 61, 63, 71–72, 124
  as liturgical source, chapter 6
Book of Common Prayer, xxv, 2, 29, 61, 63–67, 71, 84–86
  as confession of faith, 59
  the "Ornaments Rubric," 37, 64
  twentieth-century revision and the Shorter Prayer Book, 8–12, 24

calendar (liturgical), 60
Calvin, John, 59, 79–80
catechumenate
  modern, 20
  early church, 153–57
Catholic Relief Act (British legislation), 37
Chalcedon, Council of, 120
chantries, 97, 107–8
Charlemagne, Holy Roman Emperor, 120, 131, 134–38
church buildings, xxvii, 28–29, 34, 39, 89, 92, 118–19, 158
confirmation, 63
Constantine, Roman Emperor; (peace of), xxii, 118, 121–22
Cranmer, Thomas, 8, 61, 63–67
Cyril of Jerusalem, 149–50

Dante Alighieri, 88, 90, 109
devotion, private, 28, 84, 91, 96, 104–7, 109, 115, 120
Didache (Teaching of the Twelve Apostles), 146
Dix, Gregory, 143
Durkheim, Émile, 8, 35

Easter Vigil, 5, 17, 23
  Paschal Candle, 23
Edward VI, King, 65, 70
Elizabeth I, Queen, 67, 70
emerging church, xvii, xxvii
epiclesis (invocation of the Spirit), 11, 149
Eucharist (*also* Mass, Holy Communion, the Lord's Supper) 2, 5–7, 11, 19, 23, 28, 44, 50, 53, 81, 92–94, 102, 118–19, 121, 147–48
  adoration of, 70, 82–83, 89, 104
  Anglican theology of, 37, 61–62, 67–69, 70, 82–83
  communication at, 25, 69–71, 103–4, 133, 150–51
  concelebration, 20
  Jewish antecedent forms, 141–46
  Lutheran theology of, 58, 77–78
  as meal-sharing, xxii, 78, 118, 140–46
  music for, 43
  in nonliturgical churches, 12–13
  presence of Christ in, 80–81, 103, 132–34, 148
  other Protestant theology of, 56–57, 79–80
  Tridentine, 4, 7, 12, 16, 59–60, 81
  votive, 92–93

feastdays, medieval, 95, 106
Fourth Lateran Council, 133
Frankish church, 96, 121, 134–38
Frere, Walter Howard, xxiii, 3, 9, 40

Guardini, Romano, 29
Guéranger, Prosper, 31–32, 35

"Hadrianum," 137–38
Henry VIII, King, 60–61, 65, 70
Hugh of St Victor, 101
hymn, xi, 1, 17, 39, 50–51, 58, 160

inculturation (of worship), xxiv–xxv
indulgences, 76

James, William, 27
John XXIII, Pope, 13, 17–18
Justin Martyr, 147, 149–50

Latin (as language of worship), 15, 19–20, 49, 57, 61, 81, 85, 135
Liturgical Movement, xxix, 4–6, 24, chapter 2
Lumen Gentium (Dogmatic Constitution on the Church), 18
Luther, Martin, 58
  theology of, 75–78
Lyotard, Jean-François, xxiv

Mary [Tudor], Queen, 64
Mary, Blessed Virgin, 16, 25, 90, 92, 95, 109
Maskell, William, 10
Mediator Dei, papal *motu proprio*, 13–17
medievalism (movement), 28–29, 36
megachurch, xxv–xxvi
memory and worship, 115–17, 136
Migne, Jacques-Paul, 30
monasticism, 119, 123
  also Benedictine, 97, 99, 121, 126–31 (*and see* Benedict and Solesmes)
  Cluniac, 98, 120
  Dominican, 98
  Franciscan, 98
musical instruments in worship, 52–53
musicians, 51–54, 97

Nicaea, Council of, 119
Nietzsche, Friedrich, xix

Office, Divine, 7, 50–51, 60, 62–63, 66–67, 94–96, 119, 125–27, 129, 135, 151–53
  of the Dead, 107–15 (with transcription)
  Jewish antecedents, 151–52

Lutheran revision, 59
Matins, 9
Ordines Romani, 122
organ, 52
Origen, 152

Pachomius, monk, 124–27
participation (in worship, in the sacraments), xv, 1, 4–6, 8, 16, 19–22, 25, 42, 46, 59, 91, 93–96, 104, 107
as edification, 56 (*and see* Eucharist, communication at)
Passover (Jewish festival), 143–46
Peter Lombard, 101
Petrarch, Francis, 99, 109
Pius X, Pope, 4, 13–17, 25, 42–44
plainchant, revival of, 31–36, 39–43, 44–54
polyphony, 43, 48, 106
printing, 83–85
Purgatory, 75, 108

Quinones, Francisco de, cardinal, 65–67
Qumran community, 142

"reform of the reform," xxviii
revision of churches, during the English Reformation, 71–75
Ritualism (in the Church of England), 8–12, 37–39
Romanticism, xxix, 26, 31, 42, 88–89
rood-screen, 73, 96, 105, 107
rosary, 25

Sacrament Act (British legislation), 61–62
sacraments, ministers of, 102
number and constitutive features, 77, 79, 80, 82–83, 100–102
sacrifice
by Christ, 149
Jewish, 144–45
Sacrosanctum Concilium (The Constitution on the Sacred Liturgy), 18–21, 23, 42
saints, as intercessors, 63, 71, 92, 105–6
Sarum (also Salisbury), the Use of (English liturgical pattern), 10, 40–42, 65, 97 (*and see* Use, liturgical)
Second Vatican Council, xxviii–xxix, 5–6, 13–22, 25 (*and see* individual documents *Lumen Gentium*, *Sacrosanctum Concilium*)
seekers, xx
Solesmes, Abbaye-de-Saint-Pierre de, 29, 31–36, 43

Thirty-Nine Articles, 66, 70, 81–82, 85–86
Thomas Aquinas, Saint, 3, 98, 101–2, 117
Tra le sollecitudini, papal *motu proprio*, 4, 31, 42–44
translation 44–54
transubstantiation. *See* Eucharist, presence of Christ in
Trent, Council of, 4, 34, 44, 55, 59, 80–81
trope, 60

Use, liturgical (pattern of worship), 65, 97, 109, 134

Vatican II. *See* Second Vatican Council
vernacular language, xxviii, 5–6, 15, 17, 19–22, 24–25, 61, 78, 82, 84–85
vestments, 23, 70, 72

Wesley, Charles, 55, 86
Wesley, John, 8, 86
Wittgenstein, Ludwig, xi–xii, 160
women, 24, 51
worship, definitions of, xii, xiv, xvi

Zwingli, Ulrich, 79–80